FERTILITY AND FAMILY PLANNING IN THE THIRD WORLD:

A Case Study of Papua New Guinea

This study was conducted during the author's appointment in 1978–82 as United Nations Expert in Demography assigned to the Government of Papua New Guinea. The views expressed in this book are those of the author and not necessarily those of the United Nations or any of its Agencies.

FERTILITY
AND
FAMILY PLANNING
IN THE THIRD WORLD:
A Case Study of Papua New Guinea

WILLIAM K.A. AGYEI

U.N. Expert in Demography, Institute of Statistics
and Applied Economics, Makerere
University, Kampala, Uganda

CROOM HELM
London • New York • Sydney

© 1988 William K.A. Agyei
Croom Helm Ltd, Provident House,
Burrell Row, Beckenham, Kent BR3 1AT

Croom Helm Australia, 44–50 Waterloo Road,
North Ryde, 2113, New South Wales

Published in the USA by
Croom Helm
in association with Methuen, Inc.
29 West 35th Street
New York, NY 10001

British Library Cataloguing in Publication Data

Agyei, William K.A.
    Fertility and family planning in the
    third world : a case study of Papua New
    Guinea.
    1. Fertility, Human — Papua New Guinea
    2. Birth control — Papua New Guinea
    I. Title
    304.6'32'09953   HB1102.8
    ISBN 0-7099-5125-6

Library of Congress Cataloging-in-Publication Data
ISBN 0-7099-5125-6

Filmset by Mayhew Typesetting, Bristol, England
Printed and bound in Great Britain
by Billing & Sons Limited, Worcester.

Contents

Tables and Figures

FIGURES

Acknowledgements

Many people and institutions have contributed to the research project which has resulted in the publication of this book. First and foremost, I wish to acknowledge the financial support of the Population Research Programme of the Office of Environment and Conservation (Government of Papua New Guinea) and the contribution of the University of Papua New Guinea.

I am greatly indebted to Mr Gustavo Perez-Ramirez, Chief of the Population Programmes and Projects Branch at the Department of Technical Co-operation for Development, the United Nations and other colleagues in the department including Mr C. Stephen Baldwin, Mr Charles Ejiogu and Mrs Krishna Roy for their technical advice, guidance and support in the design and execution of the research project, and also for their comments on earlier drafts of certain chapters in this book. However, I wish to assure them that any mistakes or inadequacies in this book are in no way theirs, but mine alone.

Many thanks are due to Professor Richard T. Jackson, Head of the Department of Geography/Demography at the University of Papua New Guinea, for his encouragement and moral support at various stages of the research project. I am also grateful to the staff of the cartographic section of the Department for their artistic contribution to the questionnaires and maps. My thanks also go to the Printing Department at the University of Papua New Guinea for printing the questionnaires.

The field work for the research could not have succeeded without the co-operation and warm support of the national and provincial governments in the sample areas. The contribution of the news media in publicising the survey is also acknowledged. I am profoundly grateful to Mr Karol Kisokau, the Dirctor, Office of Environment and Conservation, for making it possible for some of the members of staff in the Population section to participate in the field work. I wish to thank Mrs Ruth Wylie, Miss Jan Fordham and Messrs Ovia Nou-Taboro and Jims Yaphalin for their assistance in the field work. Many thanks are due to the interviewers and supervisors; especially the demography students at the University of Papua New Guinea who worked as interviewers, coders, etc. I also wish to thank Dr Boni-Consilli Korugyendo for proof-reading the manuscript and Miss Leticia Namagembe for her skilled typing and secretarial help. Recognition is also given to the 6,391 men and women who were respondents for the survey.

Computing facilities were provided by the Department of Demography, Australian National University, Canberra, Australia and Howard University, Washington, D.C. 20059, USA. I am very grateful to Mrs J. Widdowson for helping with the initial data processing in Canberra, Mrs Maxine Dennis, Ms Lana Joyce and Mrs Clare Swift (my research officers), who worked on various stages of the research project, and Mr Kit Ronga, formerly teaching fellow at the Department of Geography, University of Papua New Guinea, for their help.

William K.A. Agyei
Kampala, Uganda

This book is dedicated to my mother, Akosua Agyebea, a woman whose efforts have enhanced the quality of my life, and to my daughter, Yvonne.

Preface

This book is based on a demographic survey of 2,923 rural and 3,360 urban male and female respondents in Papua New Guinea. The survey focused on fertility, mortality (infant and child) and family planning. The book utilises some of the current demographic techniques applicable to areas with limited data in estimating fertility, infant and child mortality measures for Papua New Guinea. It describes the fertility and mortality levels, patterns and differentials in terms of rural and urban residence, regional and educational attainment.

Chapter 1 reviews and explains demographic transition theory in the Third World. The theory proposes to explain why a society undergoing socio-economic development experiences mortality and fertility decline in a certain manner. The chapter also gives some basic background information on Papua New Guinea, such as, cultural and socio-economic organisation, demographic characteristics, family-planning activity and a review of previous demographic research works.

Chapter 2 outlines the methodology used in the research project. Details of the sample design and size, the selection of the respondents and the male and female questionnaires are given. It also discusses the organisation of the fieldwork, training of interviewers and supervisors, data collection, processing and analysis.

Chapter 3 examines some of the socio-economic and demographic characteristics of the respondents in both the rural and urban areas as well as those of the survey population in general. We found some differences and similarities between the rural and urban respondents. As expected, the occupational structure in the rural areas is oriented towards agricultural activities, while that of the urban areas is oriented towards industrial and service activities. Urban respondents have better education, higher employment status and higher incomes than their rural counterparts. The age and sex structures are similar in both areas.

Chapters 4 through 7 report findings of the research project. Considerable attention is directed towards fertility and related areas. Chapter 4 reports on breastfeeding and sexual abstinence. It was found that the main reason for prolonged breastfeeding and sexual abstinence is to ensure the welfare of the mother and child. The mean period of breastfeeding for the rural and urban mothers is similar, while there is a significant difference in the mean duration of sexual abstinence. Chapter 5 presents the results of the fertility analysis. The estimated fertility measures for the rural and urban areas of Papua New Guinea are high by world standards. Rural–urban comparison indicates that fertility is slightly lower among urban respondents. Regional and educational differences are also evident. Educational differentials are relatively significant in comparison to rural–urban and regional differentials. The results of analysis in

Chapter 6 show that infant and child mortality have declined in all parts of the country in the past 15 years prior to the survey. Infant and child mortality have been found to be slightly lower in urban areas than in rural areas, which may be attributed to the availability and easy access to health services in the urban areas. Regional differentials in infant and child mortality are more marked compared to the rural–urban differentials. In Chapter 7 we found that both the rural and urban respondents favour large families, there was a relatively high level of contraceptive awareness, but the overall practice of modern contraception in both the rural and urban areas is low. Despite the rural–urban differences in socio-economic levels, awareness of family planning is only slightly higher among the urban respondents. The level of usage of the urban respondents is slightly higher than for the rural respondents.

The concluding chapter discusses the policy implications for Papua New Guinea. The importance of the breastfeeding promotion programme and the provision of adequate family-planning services for both the rural and urban populations are stressed. It is anticipated that these measures would lead to the decline in the rate of population growth for Papua New Guinea.

1

Fertility, Family Planning and the Demographic Transition

1.1 DEMOGRAPHIC TRANSITION THEORY

Most of the Third-World countries have experienced a rapid decline in the level of mortality in the post-World-War-II era. The decline came about as a result of certain improvements in public-health services, preventive medicine and a better standard of living. Demographers and other students of population-related disciplines expected this decline to be followed by a decline in the level of fertility, following the experience of the developed countries. The stages through which the mortality–fertility declines passed are explained by demographic transition theory.[1] Basically, the theory states that both the mortality and fertility of a population will decline from high to low levels of stability as a result of socio-economic development. Furthermore, the decline in mortality usually precedes the decline in fertility. The transition process occurs in four stages. Stage one is the pre-industrial stage which is characterised by high fertility and mortality rates and in which little or no growth occurs. The second stage is one of transition or change, which is characterised by declining mortality but with fertility remaining at the traditional level, resulting in a rapid rate of population growth or a 'population explosion'. It is argued that the decline in fertility lags behind the decline in mortality because it takes time for a given population to adjust to the fact that the mortality rate really is lower, and because the social and economic institutions that favoured a high fertility level require time to adjust to new norms of lower fertility that are more consistent with a lower level of mortality. Most of the Third-World countries are in this stage. In stage three the fertility rate gradually declines on account of the weakening of pronatal, traditional institutions for fewer children. The fourth stage is characterised by both very low mortality and fertility rates when the idea of conscious control of fertility embraces the whole society and the use of

---

[1] See for example, W.S. Thompson, 1929; F.W. Notestein, 1953; D.O. Cowgill, 1963).

contraception is widespread. This is the stage of zero rate of natural increase and accordingly, the population gets back into a stable state.

The pattern of demographic transition in the Third-World countries is different from that of the developed countries. Mortality levels fell rapidly when medical and public-health services were introduced, the use of antibiotics and vaccinations reduced the number of deaths from infectious diseases, the use of insecticides helped to control malaria. These changes did not result from socio-economic development within the various countries of the Third World but were 'imported' through technical or foreign aid. In stage two of the demographic transition in the Third World, fertility levels have remained high and even increased in some of the countries as a result of the better health enjoyed by the population. With declining mortality and high fertility levels, the rate of population growth reached 2.2 per cent per year in the 1960s. Since 1970 the fertility rate in certain parts of the Third World has fallen, and the fertility rate of the Third World as a whole has declined by 26 per cent, from 42 per 1000 in 1970 to 31 per 1000 in 1985. This pattern of decline in mortality–fertility levels has led some researchers to question whether the demographic transition theory is applicable in the Third World. Others discount the theory on the grounds that it does not generate explanations for observed demographic phenomena (see for example, Agyei, 1978; Beaver, 1975; Oechsli and Kirk, 1975;. Teitelbaum, 1975, etc.).

A number of demographers hold the view that socio-economic development with its fundamental changes in the status of women and in the economic value of children is the only possible basis for the transition from high to low fertility levels (see for example, Davis, 1967, 1973; Ryder, 1976). Some economists noted that socio-economic development programmes would be more successful if the very high fertility levels could be reduced, thereby providing more productive sort of capital investment (Coale and Hoover, 1958). Other demographers, social planners and policy makers felt that the high level of fertility in Third-World countries could be reduced through the intervention of organised family-planning programmes. It was argued that any country at any level of socio-economic development could reduce its level of fertility, thereby slowing down the rate of population growth so as to permit development programmes to advance more rapidly than they would if the level of fertility was high. This idea was the cornerstone for family-planning programmes that were introduced by private organisations and governments in the early 1950s and 1960s.

1.2 FAMILY PLANNING IN THE THIRD WORLD

The adoption of a family-planning policy in the Third-World countries started with India in 1952. The People's Republic of China and Hong Kong followed in 1956. By 1959, only five countries (India, China, Hong Kong, Tonga and

Taiwan) had family-planning policies and as late as 1963 only eleven countries had adopted such policies. All of the eleven countries were in the Asia–Pacific region with the exception of Cuba in the Latin America–Caribbean region. There were no such policies in Africa, Central or South America or the Middle East. However, in 1965, with seven more countries adopting family-planning policies, the pace increased and continued to rise steadily into the early 1980s. By the end of 1981, 41 of the 44 countries in the Third World with populations of ten million or more were supporting the policy of family planning. The only exceptions were Burma, Saudi Arabia and Argentina.

The proportion of the population in Third-World countries with government policies supportive of family planning jumped from zero to 22 per cent with its adoption by India in 1952 and to 51 per cent with its adoption by China in 1956 (Watson, 1975); thereafter the rate increased gradually and by the end of 1982 reached about 96 per cent — in 85 Third-World countries each with a national policy. In 42 of these countries the national policy had a demographic objective; i.e. to slow down the rate of population growth in order to enhance the prospects for rapid socio-economic growth. And in 43 countries, the family-planning policy had a health and human-rights objective (World Bank, 1984).

The sharp diversity in economic, social, cultural and political settings in the Third-World countries influences demographic changes as well as the formulation of family-planning policy, or for that matter population policy in general. In view of this diversity, the regional patterns in terms of family-planning policy are striking. According to Watson (1975), it began in South Asia with India in 1952. By 1960 with its adoption by Pakistan–Bangladesh, 97 per cent of the region's population lived in countries with family-planning policies and by 1966 the figure was more than 99 per cent. The policy was adopted later in East Asia — in 1956 by China and Hong Kong — and by 1961, 98 per cent of the population of this region lived in areas with such a policy. Family-planning policies did not develop in Southeast Asia until 1962 when North Vietnam adopted a policy and was joined by Thailand and Indonesia between 1967–68. In Oceania, Tonga adopted a policy in 1958, followed by Fiji in 1962, Papua New Guinea in 1968 and Western Samoa and the Solomon Islands in 1970.

The trend in Latin America and the Caribbean was much slower. Cuba adopted a policy in the early 1960s and was followed by most Latin American countries between 1964 and 1969. But these policies embraced only 56 per cent of the population in the region and it was not until 1974 that this figure increased to over 90 per cent when Mexico and Brazil adopted policies in 1972 and 1974 respectively. In the Middle East and North Africa, family-planning policies were not initiated until 1964, beginning with Tunisia. Egypt, Morocco and Turkey followed in 1965. Even today, a number of countries in this region have not adopted family planning policies.

The situation in the Sub-Saharan region of Africa is quite different. Kenya was the first among the Anglophone countries to adopt a policy in 1966 (as did South Africa). Policies became more widespread in the 1970s and by 1974 about

95 per cent of the population were covered. Among the Francophone countries of Sub-Saharan Africa only the small island of Réunion adopted a family-planning policy in 1966. Mali and Benin followed in 1972, Zaïre in 1973, Cameroon and Togo in 1975 and Senegal and the Republic of the Congo in 1976. Even now, a number of these French-speaking African countries have not adopted family-planning policies.

1.3 FAMILY-PLANNING SERVICES

It must be pointed out that the adoption of a family-planning policy does not necessarily imply ready access to government or even private-sector family-planning services. For example, in India family-planning services developed rather slowly after its adoption in 1952. This was also the case in Bangladesh. The pace was more rapid in Hong Kong, South Korea, Taiwan and Fiji. According to Watson (1975) by 1965, government family-planning services were established in about 12 to 14 countries in the Third World. Currently, more than 50 countries have well-established family-planning services.

On a regional basis, public family-planning services are at different levels of development in different regions of the Third World. The World Bank (1984) published some information which is summarised below:

East Asia: Governments in this region have a long-standing commitment to reduce population growth. And they have been extremely successful in improving easy access to family-planning services as well as in providing a wide range of contraceptives. In addition, large numbers of field workers have been employed to provide family planning, and sometimes basic health care, in villages in China, Indonesia and Thailand.

South Asia: Official commitment to reduce fertility is strong, but results have been mixed. Use of contraceptives is highest in Sri Lanka and several states in southern India and is lowest in Nepal and Pakistan. The wide use of contraception is hampered by high infant mortality and by the preference for large families. Most of the programmes have not matched those of East Asia in reaching the rural population.

Latin America and the Caribbean: In the two decades preceding the 1970s, a widespread demand for family planning was met in the private sector. Government support was weak because of opposition from the church. Most governments now support and provide family-planning services for health and humanitarian purposes. Some governments such as Barbados, Colombia, the Dominican Republic, El Salvador, Guatamala, Haiti, Jamaica, Mexico and Trinidad and Tobago do so to reduce fertility as well. Access to services in rural areas is still inadequate in most countries of the region.

Middle East and North Africa: Some countries in North Africa, for example, Egypt, Morocco and Tunisia, have long-established programmes to reduce fertility. About half the countries provides family-planning services to improve child spacing and to promote health; only Turkey's programme seeks to reduce fertility. In a few Middle Eastern countries, contraception is illegal. In others, cultural practices often confine women to their households, which makes it difficult for them to seek out family-planning services.

Sub-Saharan Africa: Among the 41 countries for which data is available, only nine provide family-planning services to reduce fertility. Most governments that support family planning do so for health reasons and there are still twelve countries with no official backing for family planning. Services are provided through health care systems and have limited coverage, particularly in rural areas. Contraceptive use is not widespread as infant mortality is high and throughout Africa couples want large families.

Oceania: Of the five countries which provide some data on family-planning services, Fiji provides the most extensive services. Tonga and Western Samoa also provide adequate services. Services are improving in Papua New Guinea and the Solomon Islands.

1.4 DEMOGRAPHIC TRANSITION IN THE THIRD WORLD

The data presented in Table 1.1 for some selected Third-World countries reveals that most of them are undergoing the demographic transition. Mortality levels have declined in all the Third-World countries and the pace of the decline compared to the historical experience of the now developed countries has been rapid over two or three decades. The source of the decline, as pointed out earlier, is largely due to imported health and medical technology and not related to socio-economic development. When mortality began to decline in many of the Third-World countries, the level of socio-economic development was not comparable with those levels prevailing in Western Europe before the Industrial Revolution (World Bank, 1972).

Fertility levels in most of the Third-World countries are much higher than in pretransition Western Europe because of the early and almost universal marriage pattern. In contrast, the pattern of late marriage and non-marriage was quite common in Europe at that time. There is strong evidence that fertility has started to decline in some of the Third-World countries at quite different levels of socio-economic development (see Table 1.1). In the fifteen-year period from 1950 to 1965 according to Mauldin (1978), the declines in fertility in the Third-World countries were limited to a few small countries. The tempo of the decline increased during the next ten years, with 19 countries of half a million or more having fertility declines in excess of 20 per cent. More importantly, ten countries of the 13 Third-World countries with populations of 35 million or more reported significant declines in their crude birth rate (CBR). Beaver (1975) has noted that Latin American and Caribbean countries that have experienced fertility declines in recent decades have shown a more rapid rate of decline than that which occurred in 19th-century Europe.

Table 1.1: Demographic and fertility-related indicators for selected countries 1960 and 1985

Region and country	Population in millions		Crude birth rate		Crude death rate		Total fertility rate		Family planning index[b]
	1960[a]	1985	1960	1985	1960	1985	1960[a]	1985	
Sub-Saharan Africa									
Kenya	8.1	20.2	55.0	54.0	24.0	13.0	6.8	8.0	D
Tanzania	10.3	21.7	47.0	50.0	22.0	15.0	6.4	7.1	D
Nigeria	43.0	91.2	52.2	48.0	25.0	17.0	7.0	6.3	E
Zaire	14.1	33.1	48.0	45.0	24.0	16.0	5.8	6.1	E
Sudan	11.9	21.8	47.0	46.0	25.0	17.0	6.3	6.6	E
Ethiopia	20.7	36.0	51.0	43.0	28.0	22.0	—[c]	6.7	E
Middle East and North Africa									
Egypt	26.0	48.3	42.9	37.0	20.0	10.0	6.0	5.3	D
Morocco	11.6	24.3	50.0	41.0	21.0	12.0	6.7	5.9	D
Turkey	27.5	52.1	43.0	35.0	16.0	10.0	5.8	5.1	D
Algeria	10.8	22.2	43.4	45.0	20.0	12.0	7.1	7.0	D
Latin America and Caribbean									
Colombia	14.6	29.4	47.0	28.0	17.0	7.0	5.8	3.6	B
Cuba	6.8	10.1	31.7	16.0	9.0	6.0	4.0	1.8	C
Mexico	36.0	79.7	45.0	32.0	12.0	6.0	6.1	5.9	B
Brazil	70.9	138.4	43.0	31.0	13.0	8.0	—	4.0	C
Venezuela	7.4	17.3	45.9	33.0	11.0	6.0	5.8	4.1	D
Peru	10.0	19.5	47.0	35.0	19.0	10.0	5.5	5.2	D

South Asia									
Sri Lanka	9.9	16.4	36.6	27.0	9.0	6.0	4.3	3.7	B
India	429.0	762.2	48.0	34.0	24.0	13.0	5.7	4.5	B
Bangladesh	—	101.5	47.0	45.0	22.0	17.0	—	6.4	C
Pakistan	—	99.2	49.0	43.0	23.0	15.0	—	6.4	C
Nepal	9.4	17.0	46.0	42.0	26.0	18.0	6.1	6.3	D
East Asia									
China	636.0	1,042.0	39.0	19.0	24.0	8.0	4.0	2.1	A
Korea, Rep. of	24.9	42.7	43.0	23.0	14.0	6.0	4.1	2.6	A
Indonesia	94.2	168.4	44.2	34.0	23.0	12.0	5.8	4.4	B
Malaysia	9.3	15.7	44.0	29.0	15.0	7.0	5.9	4.0	B
Thailand	26.4	52.7	34.7	25.0	15.0	6.0	5.0	3.9	C
Philippines	27.4	56.8	47.0	32.0	15.0	7.0	6.5	4.8	C
Singapore	1.6	2.6	38.7	16.0	6.0	5.0	2.8	1.7	A
Oceania									
Fiji	0.4	0.7	39.9	31.0	6.6	6.0	5.0	3.6	C
New Caledonia	0.1	0.2	34.1	25.0	8.7	6.0	5.4	3.6	—
Papua New Guinea	1.9	3.3	44.0	40.0	23.0	14.0	6.1	6.0	D
Western Samoa	0.1	0.2	—	34.0	—	8.0	—	4.9	D
Solomon Islands	0.1	0.3	38.7	43.0	—	12.0	—	7.2	—

Notes: a. 1960 Population figures were taken from UN Demographic Yearbooks, 1963, 1964 and 1965.

b. A = very strong; B = strong; C = moderate; D = weak; E = very weak or none

c. Not available.

Sources: World Bank, World Development Report, 1984; Figures for 1985 are taken from 1985 World Population Data Sheet, Population Reference Bureau, Washington, DC.

In a recent analysis of conditions of fertility decline in 94 Third-World countries, Mauldin and Berelson (1978) identified three religious and cultural factors which are associated with high fertility levels: (1) the Catholic Church, on doctrinal grounds; (2) Islam, through subordination of women in the cultural traditions; and (3) Black Africa, because of the traditional status of women within the society. It is worth noting that Middle Eastern and Sub-Saharan Muslim countries exhibit less of a decline than the rest of the Third-World countries.

1.5 DEMOGRAPHIC CHANGES IN SINGAPORE AND CHINA

Singapore and China are two countries that are fundamentally different but serve to illustrate the possible independent effect of high population pressure and very strong government supported family-planning programmes organised to reach the masses. While the data from China may be questionable, the two countries deserve special attention because of the level of socio-economic development in each country and the method by which each is undergoing the demographic transition.

Singapore is a country which is probably going through the stages of demographic transition under the normal conditions. In 1960, its crude birth rate was approximately 39 per 1000 and the crude death rate was 6 per 1000. By 1985, the crude birth rate had declined to 16 per 1000, the crude death rate to 5 per 1000 and its total fertility rate was 1.7 per woman. Even by 1975, Singapore's net reproduction rate was 0.97, i.e. below replacement level. Singapore is the first Third-World country to undergo the transition from a high to a low level of fertility. However, it must be pointed out that this decline (according to Watson, 1975) occurred in the context of interaction between rapid socio-economic development on the one hand and a comprehensive family-planning programme on the other.

The transition from high to low fertility in Singapore took a little over two decades. In 1957 the total fertility was 6.5. It dropped to 4.5 in 1965 — the date of the introduction of the family-planning programme — and by 1969 to 3.2. The family-planning programme in Singapore had very strong governmental support and featured a mix of advocating sterilisation, the use of the pill and condoms and a strong postpartum and postabortal recruitment effort. Abortion was legalised in 1969 and the laws were liberalised in 1974. There is no doubt that the family-planning programme might have accelerated the decline in fertility which fell rapidly by about 62 per cent betwen 1965 and 1982. Apart from the effective family-planning methods used, the programme also included an excellent information/education effort, a vigorous 'Stop at Two' campaign as well as home visits and even telephone follow-ups!

It is important to point out that Singapore's successful family-planning programme may be difficult to replicate in other Third-World countries.

Singapore is 100 per cent urban, has a small population of 2.6 million (1985 estimate), excellent health services, a high *per capita* income, low infant mortality, good sources of data, a high rate of institutional births and abortions and has developed very rapidly.

China (the People's Republic of) will probably be the first large country to experience the transition from high mortality and fertility levels to low mortality and fertility levels in the Third World. China is experiencing very dramatic demographic changes — its crude birth rate declined from 39 per 1000 in 1960 to 19 per 1000 in 1985. The crude death rate also declined from 24 per 1000 to 8 per 1000 during the same period. The total fertility rate declined from 7.5 children to 2.3 per woman in 1985 and is expected to fall to approximately 2.0 by the year 2000.

The current official population policy promotes later marriage, longer spacing between births, reduced marital fertility and fewer children. In the early 1970s, China made the greatest use of measures to promote small families. The slogan then was 'One is the best, two you square the account, three you make a mistake'. Sometimes the Chinese have relied on individual incentives such as giving priority in housing schemes to parents with only two children. In the late 1970s, it became clear that with the large number of women entering childbearing age as a result of past high fertility and declining mortality, even compliance with a two-child family as the norm would not reduce China's rate of population growth enough to meet the national goal of 1.2 billion people by the year 2000.

In 1979, the province of Sichuan instituted a policy designed to persuade married couples to have no more than one child. This policy was backed by a system of economic rewards to parents with more than one child who committed themselves to have no more, and penalties for those who had more than two. This soon became a national policy and individual provinces are all expected to implement such systems. In 1980 the Vice Premier stated as specific goals that 95 per cent of married couples in the cities and 90 per cent in the rural areas should have only one child (World Bank, 1984). By 1982, most provinces and municipalities in China had introduced incentives and disincentives to promote the one-child norm.

However, several factors are working against the one-child policy. The World Bank (1984) has identified four main factors: (1) security in old age — a compulsory pension system applies only to employees in state enterprises in urban areas who constitute only 15 per cent of the labour force. For the rural majority, children remain the main source of security in old age. (2) The responsibility system — the widespread introduction of the production responsibility system has given families a direct economic incentive to have more children for two reasons. In some areas, land for household use is allocated on a *per capita* basis, so having more children ensures access to more land. In addition, security for the elderly is provided on a collective basis which will be reduced as collective income declines. In an effort to combat this, some brigades have introduced a double contracting system under which households are required both to deliver their quota of farm output to the state and to refrain from having an unauthorized birth. (3) Persistent male preference — a preference for sons is a strong cultural impediment to having only one child. The pressure to have one child (and the desire for a boy) may have led to a revival of the practice of female infanticide, about which the Chinese government has expressed considerable concern. The 1982 census revealed that the sex ratio at birth for 1981 was 108.5, an abnormally high figure. (4) Financing incentives — responsibility for financing incentives falls on local areas and not on the central government. As a result there is great variation in the type and value of incentives.

The experiences of Singapore and China demonstrate that a decline in fertility could be achieved within the context of a rapidly growing socio-economic development and a very strong family-planning programme as in the case of Singapore. And it can also be achieved in low-income economies with a very strong government support for a family-planning programme as in the case of China. Accordingly, high levels of socio-economic development are not a necessary condition for fertility decline.

It is therefore possible for a country such as Papua New Guinea, which is classified in the lower middle-income group (World Bank, 1984), to undergo the transition from a high fertility level to a low fertility level if there is very strong government support for a family-planning programme. Mortality has declined since World War II, and although there is scope for a further decline in mortality (particularly among infants and children) fertility has not shown any signs of declining. The family-planning programme in Papua New Guinea is a weak one, and as such has no impact on the fertility level. This report, which is based on the analysis of data collected in a demographic survey (details in Chapter 2), focuses mainly on fertility and fertility-related areas as well as mortality. However, because of the nature of the data, estimates of mortality are calculated using indirect techniques and are limited to infant and child mortality. The results of our analysis might be used more appropriately as a framework for building hypotheses about how various attitudes concerning fertility and family planning are formed and how the problems are to be faced and solved in providing a very strong government-supported family-planning programme for the people of Papua New Guinea.

1.6 PAPUA NEW GUINEA: THE LAND AND ITS PEOPLE

Papua New Guinea (see Figure 1) lies wholly within the tropics and is commonly described as the eastern half of the world's second largest island, the western half being the Indonesian section of Irian Jaya. The country also consists, in the east, of a few large and many smaller scattered islands of the Bismark and Louisade Archipelagoes and the North Solomon islands. Papua New Guinea comprises an area of about 474,000 square kilometres — about the same area as Thailand. The country contains some of the world's most rugged land

Figure 1: Papua New Guinea

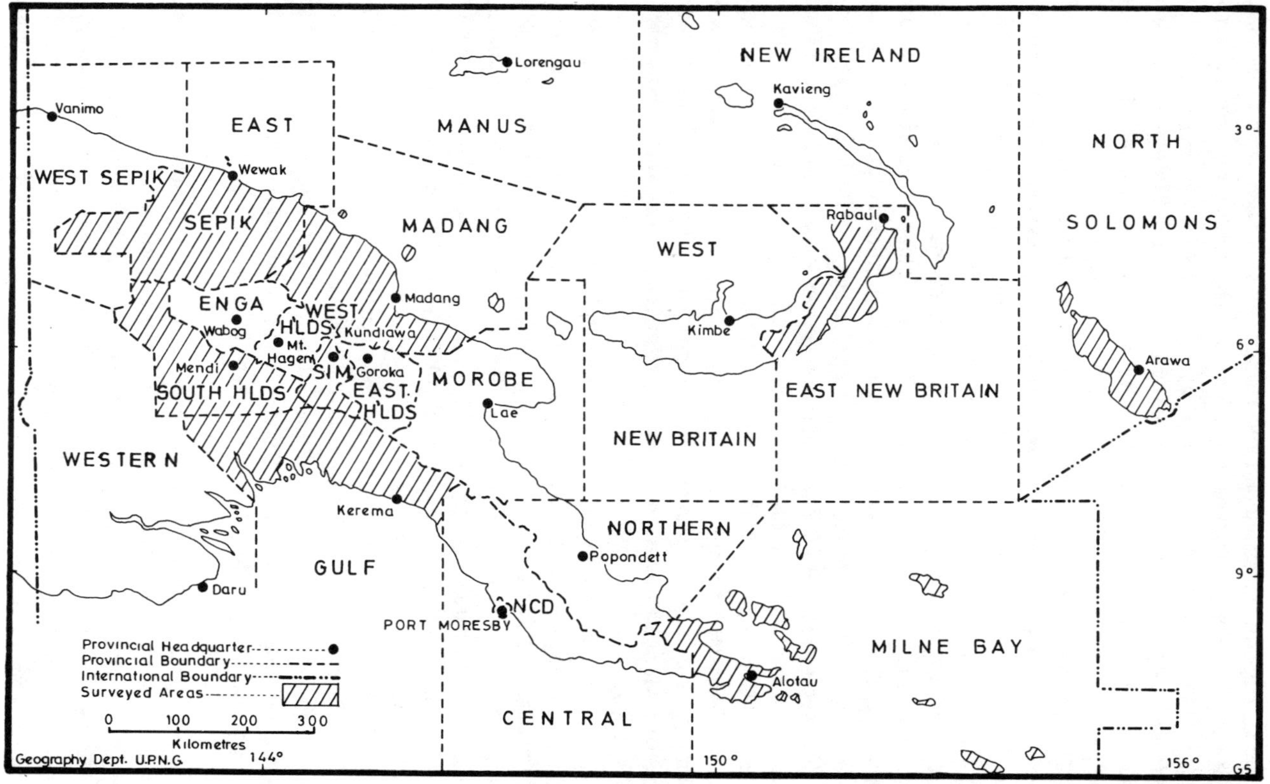

NORTH SOLOMONS

Arawa

NEW IRELAND

Kavieng

Rabaul

EAST NEW BRITAIN

WEST

Kimbe

NEW BRITAIN

MILNE BAY

Alotau

NORTHERN

Popondett

Lorengau

MANUS

MADANG

Madang

WEST HLDS

Kundiawa

Goroka

SIM EAST HLDS

Mt. Hagen

Wabag

EAST SEPIK

Wewak

ENGA

Mendi

SOUTH HLDS

Vanimo

WEST SEPIK

MOROBE

Lae

NCD

PORT MORESBY

CENTRAL

GULF

Kerema

WESTERN

Daru

Provincial Headquarter
Provincial Boundary
International Boundary
Surveyed Areas

Kilometres

0   100   200   300

Geography Dept. U.P.N.G.

3°
6°
9°

156°

150°

144°

11 PNG 43....3.80

G5

features. High and rugged mountains rising over 4,000 metres (the highest peak is Mount Wilhelm at 4,519 metres), thick forests, vast swamps and large rivers and the many islands divide the country into one whose ecology is as diverse and varied as can be found in any other part of the world. These physical barriers have undoubtedly led to the wide cultural and linguistic diversity found among the people.

The climate is equatorial with high average temperatures and humidity. A predominant seasonal feature is the regular alternation between two major air streams: the southeast trade winds (which prevail from May to October) and the northwest monsoon (from November to April) causing an alternating 'dry' and 'wet' seasonal pattern. In the coastal areas of the mainland and in the islands this pattern is quite noticeable. In general, the highlands experience far cooler temperatures and have a less definite seasonal variation in rainfall. Frosts occur in the highlands, sometimes causing crop damage and food shortages.

The people are classified with the Melanesian stock of the Western Pacific, but smaller admixtures of Micronesian stock occur around the Admiralty Islands. There are about 700 discrete languages, classified into Austronesian, mainly a coastal language group, and non-Austronesian which is the predominant language of the Highlands. Pidgin is spoken widely throughout the country and Hiri Motu is spoken along the coast of Papua. English is, however, the official language.

Social organisation in Papua New Guinea is based on the clan system, whose members range from a few hundreds in lowland areas to thousands in some parts of the Highlands. Strathern (1971: 23) points to the clan level as being of 'central importance in political action'. The clan is egalitarian, with position in the society being related to acquired rather than to inherited status (Hastings 1973: 16–17) except in some Papua and Sepik societies where there are hereditary chieftains. Land ownership is vested in the clan or in smaller kinship groups. Life for the most part is based on autonomous local groups called 'parishes', being villages on the coast or hamlets in the Highlands. Food is usually obtained from subsistence farming, and the method of farming is that of shifting agriculture. Staple foods on the coast, such as yams and taro, are supplemented by fish and in the Highlands the sweet potato is the main food. Other root crops and 'greens' form part of the diet, together with bananas. Coconut is a basic cooking ingredient on the mainland coasts and on the islands. Sago flour is also used. Fish, pork, beef and mutton (from Australia and New Zealand) and poultry provide the protein content to an otherwise largely vegetarian diet.

Economic organisation in Papua New Guinea — that is, the need for an efficient division of labour — seems to dictate the size of parishes which are, in turn, dependent upon the ecology of the particular area. Divisions of labour, in the main, are based on age and sex, although there was in the past some specialisation according to the need for essential items which were obtained through trading: salt, pigs, tobacco, canoes, pots, sago, etc. (For example, the Siane considered that one salt cake was worth one pig.) Cash cropping of vegetable and export crops has, in some instances, drawn away much labour from subsistence farming. The cash received from coffee, cocoa, copra, rubber, or money earned from selling in food markets is increasingly used to buy imported foods like tinned fish and meat, rice and biscuits. These foods are becoming the staple diet of those with a cash income in Papua New Guinea. It is interesting to note, however, that the exchange of traditional foods and other items continues to play an integral part in the social and economic activities. Exchanges validate different stages of the life cycle, like marriage and initiation; they represent the core of compensation and the strengthening of political alliances — for example, Moka in the Western Highlands and Enga.

Social behaviour within Papua New Guinean societies is, to a large extent, regulated by traditional beliefs in magic, sorcery, the spirits of the ancestors and in places and objects. These beliefs still influence the day-to-day behaviour of men and women, especially in small rural communities. The impact of introduced institutions like churches, formal education, health services, agriculture and economic development is gradually leading to the abandonment of many traditional beliefs and practices although 'puri puri' (magic) is still a very real phenomenon in many rural and/or traditional communities. These factors — combined with rural–urban migration by many in search of employment, the desire to escape traditional obligations and authority and the wish to acquire marketable skills — have radically changed the pattern of life in many villages.

1.7 DEMOGRAPHIC CHARACTERISTICS

The population of Papua New Guinea according to the 1980 census is approximately 3.1 million. Its demographic characteristics are similar to those of many other Third-World countries; the population is growing rapidly, is disproportionately young and is predominantly rural and agricultural. The rate of population growth between 1966 and 1971 was 2.6 per cent per year and the preliminary results of the 1980 census suggest a lower growth rate of 2.1 per cent per year. If this growth rate continues, the population will exceed twice its present number within the next 35 years. The high growth rate, unprecedented in Papua New Guinea's past demographic history, is the result of the population's recent history of declining mortality in the face of its persistently high level of fertility. According to the 1980 census, 47 per cent of the population are under the age of 15 and the median age (half over, half under) of the population was about 14.6. The median ages of the population in 1966 and 1971 were 19.1 and 17.6 years respectively. As a result, Papua New Guinea is characterised by a high youth-dependency ratio, and each year there are large and growing numbers of children to be fed, clothed, educated and otherwise cared for.

Papua New Guinea is also one of the least urbanised countries within the

Third World (for detailed discussion of the levels and rates of urbanisation in Papua New Guinea see Agyei, 1982). According to the 1980 census, 89 per cent of the population lived in rural areas. Nevertheless, the country is now experiencing a trend toward urbanisation. The proportion of the population living in urban areas has been increasing steadily in the past 14 years. The level of urban growth increased from 4 per cent in 1966 to 8 per cent in 1971 and was 11 per cent in 1980.

The youthful nature of the population affects the age structure. Although absolute numbers present the most immediate measure of any nation's population problem, the age structure of a given population has demographic and economic consequences that can affect the severity of those problems in terms of the economic and social development of certain areas and the amount of employment available at the different levels of formal education. The main factors which determine the age structure are:

(1) the level of fertility — a high fertility level or an increase in the number of births will produce a young population;
(2) the level of mortality — a decline in the number of deaths favours the young in the Third-World countries where infant- and child-mortality rates are high;
(3) migration — generally undertaken by young adults, results in a younger population in the receiving area.

Facotrs (1) and (2) above are operative in Papua New Guinea from the results of the available data. Fertility appears to remain constant at the 1966 level. It is very unlikely that fertility might have increased between 1966 and 1974, as the United Nations Fund for Population Activities (UNFPA) funded family-planning project started in 1974. The following reasons may account for the probable increase in fertility levels:

1. In the past it was common practice in many parts of the country for taboos to be placed on relations between husbands and wives. This was especially true after childbirth for long periods of time (i.e. during the lactation period) which may be one or two years, although this did not apply to all areas of Papua New Guinea. For example, in Motuan society men and women share the same house. Whatever the situation, people were conscious of the need for child spacing. With the influence of Western culture, initially through missions, these taboos and traditions are collapsing because they are perceived as being 'primitive'. This concept, however, tends to apply mainly to urban areas or to those places with easy access to urban centres. Also, although most urban dwellers would prefer fewer children the mode of living in urban areas (that is, forcing men and women to share the same house with limited space in many cases) would seem to contribute to the increase in the level of fertility.

2. The mere fact that changes in the age structure leading to a young

14

population is in itself evidence that may suggest an increase in the fertility level.

There is no doubt that mortality continues to decline from the 1971 level (17.0 deaths per 1000 in the midyear population), particularly infant and child mortality as improvements in the health infrastructure, education, communications and standard of living are being made.

Although migration is taking place, emigration is minimal according to the available data. The migration process taking place in Papua New Guinea is internal and has no influence on population growth or on the age structure of the population as a whole. However, rural-to-urban migration of large numbers of school-leavers and young job seekers, has caused a significant imbalance in the age and sex structures in cities like Port Moresby and Lae. In recent years Papua New Guinea experienced a movement of people from other parts of the country to the copper-mining areas of the North Solomon Islands (Bougainville and Buka) and to the cocoa and copra plantations of East New Britain to seek employment; that movement seems to have levelled off at the moment. Nevertheless, the regular movement from rural to urban areas continues and this is clearly evident in the works of Skeldon (1980) and Agyei (1982a).

1.8 FAMILY-PLANNING PROGRAMME IN PAPUA NEW GUINEA

Voluntary family-planning activities started in Papua New Guinea in the early 1960s with the founding of the Family Welfare Association in Port Moresby in 1961 (Bowler, 1968). Family-planning clinics were established in Port Moresby in 1962 and in Kainantu in 1967. The Association became affiliated with the International Planned Parenthood Federation (IPPF) in 1974, and is now known as the Family Planning Association of Papua New Guinea. It is currently funded by the IPPF and provides limited family-planning services. It has, however, taken the initiative in setting up a scheme for community-based distribution of condoms, to be followed at a later date by the social marketing of oral contraceptives.

It was the policy of the (Australian) colonial administration to provide family-planning assistance when requested. According to the Five-Year Plan (Territory of Papua New Guinea 1968), 'it is proposed to make family-planning services increasingly available in both urban and rural areas'. In 1967 the government decided to make family planning a health-related activity under the Department of Public Health.

The family-planning activities within the Department of Public Health are concerned with the improvement and welfare of the family, particularly involving pregnancy, and include the spacing of children, regulating the size of the famliy, helping sub-fertile couples to have children and providing information and counselling on matters related to parenthood. The family-planning services

15

are restricted only to married women (those legally married or to those in common-law union).

Currently, the family-planning services provided by the Department of Public Health are funded by the United Nations Fund for Population Activities (UNFPA) with an initial budget of 302,252 US dollars for the period 1974 to 1976. The government, however, provides the salaries of the personnel involved in the delivery of family planning services. There are 145 family-planning clinics in Papua New Guinea, each having either a medical officer, a trained nurse, a health extension officer or, in a few cases, aid-post orderlies (APOs) in charge who are supervised in the field by the provincial health officer and his/her staff. The strategy is to integrate family-planning services with maternal and child health and general health services.

Field-work operations were given priority from the outset of the programme. The primary functions of the field workers are to educate women about contraception and motivate them to accept family planning. Operations in the field are carried out by aid-post orderlies, health education officers and staff responsible for maternal- and child-health care; the assistance of influential persons in various communities is solicited. According to (Rafiq, n.d.), no deliberate incentives or disincentives to promote public acceptance of family planning are employed.

For the public, education and information are provided by the Department of Public Health personnel (maternal- and child-health nurses). In addition, the office of Environment and Conservation, the Office of Information, the Departments of Education and Primary Industries and the National Broadcasting Commission are encouraged to create an awareness of the interrelationships of population growth, development and social and economic welfare.

The government's family-planning services offer a wide range of contraceptives which include the pill, an injection of Depo-provera, intrauterine devices, condoms, ovulation/rhythm, tubal ligation and vasectomy. Aid-post orderlies and supervisors distribute condoms and pills in the rural areas. All services and supplies carry a charge which ranges from five toea[2] (about 7 US cents) per condom to five kina[2] (K5.00) (about 7 US dollars) for a Depo-provera injection. Fees are much lower, however, than those charged by doctors in private practice.

The family-planning programmes appear to concentrate their efforts in the urban centres of Papua New Guinea because of the concentration of facilities and health personnel in these areas. Efforts are also being made to promote the programme in the rural areas, but lack of trained personnel is a limiting factor.

The numbers using contraceptives (acceptors) have increased rather slowly and irregularly from under 2,500 in the period 1967 to 1968 slightly over 15,000 in 1980 (see Table 1.2).

---

[2] K1.00 was equivalent to 1.50 US dollars at the time of the survey (100 toeas = K1.00).

Table 1.2: Acceptors of family planning in Papua New Guinea 1967/68–1981

Year	Number of new acceptors	Cumulative number of acceptors	Acceptors as a percentage of women 15–49 years old	Cumulative percentage of acceptors
1967–68	2,299	2,299	0.43	0.43
1968–69	2,050	4,349	0.38	0.81
1969–70	1,773	6,122	0.38	1.14
1970–71	1,756	7,878	0.32	1.46
1971–72	2,725	10,603	0.49	1.95
1972–73	3,491	14,094	0.62	2.57
1973–74	5,427	19,521	0.95	3.52
1974–75	7,394	26,915	1.28	4.80
1975–76	10,118	37,033	1.73	6.53
1976[a]	9,789	46,822	1.66	8.19
1977	13,294	60,116	2.23	10.42
1978	11,614	71,730	1.92	12.34
1979	11,835	83,565	1.93	14.27
1980[b]	15,325	98,890	2.48	16.75
1981[b]	14,901	113,791	2.38	19.13

Sources: 1967–68 to 1975–76 derived from Muirden, 1976.
1976–81 Department of Public Health, Family Health and Family-Planning Programme.

Notes: a. Reporting of new acceptors changed to calendar year.
b. Provisional data.

Acceptors as a proportion of all women of reproductive age were generally under 1 per cent in the period 1973 to 1974, averaged 1.8 per cent from 1974–5 to 1979 and reached 2.5 per cent in 1980. On the basis of the data presented in Table 1.2, family-planning services have reached approximately 19 per cent of the target population.

There is no doubt that the execution of a successful family-planning programme in Papua New Guinea would encounter major obstacles with respect both to demand and supply of services. Contributing to the low demand is the combination of low levels of literacy and a predominantly agrarian way of life. But Rafiq's surveys (1977, 1978) in the Northern, Central and Eastern Highlands Provinces indicate that levels of literacy are not as important with regard to the use of contraceptives as is their continuity of supply — and this is the major obstacle. Surveys carried out in Morocco and Honduras (The Population Council, October and September, 1970, respectively) give similar findings.

In this respect, the supply of contraceptives in Papua New Guinea, especially of clinically-based methods, would have to overcome formidable difficulties due to the physical nature of the country. Other factors which produce obstacles to a successful family-planning programme, are the shortage of suitably qualified medical personnel of all levels and the pressing need for primary health care, which universally takes precedence over family planning in the priorities of those trained in and committed to curative medicine. However, family planning could be considered and offered to the public as a form of 'preventive medicine' — as a part of primary health care — and should form an integral part of training courses for all medical personnel. Against these odds, the absence of an official population policy is perhaps a handicap of secondary importance.

Also, before family planning was introduced, no studies had been conducted that explored the awareness, knowledge, attitude and practice of contraception (traditional or conventional) among the indigenous population. The only studies in this area available are those of Rafiq (1977, 1978), and these were limited to three rural areas.

1.9 PRIOR RESEARCHES

Research activities into fertility and mortality rates in Papua New Guinea have been limited to small areas of the population based on the argument that each area or population group is quite different from any other area. This is a valid argument, but there are also similarities which can form a basis for intelligent analysis of the subject. Most of these researches were carried out by medical officers and anthropologists before the 1950s. The theme of these researchers was basically that of depopulation. For example, Dempwolff (1904) studied the Western Islands while Kopp (1913) dealt with the situation in New Britain just before World War I. Later, other researchers, including Murray (1925),

Williams (1932/33) and Vial (1937/38), concentrated their work on the mainland whereas Cilento (1923, 1924, 1928), Jackson (1924), Chinnery (1926, 1931, 1932/33), Bellamy (1926), Powdermaker (1931) and Holland (1931) all carried out their research on the archipelagos.

World War II interrupted further demographic research until the early 1950s when another crop of researchers, again having depopulation as their main topic and the New Guinea Islands as their main concern, began population-related research. The work included the unpublished research of Refshauge (1950), and Gregory (1955) and the published work of Scragg (1957).

After the late 1950s the focus of research took a new dimension. Depopulation ceased to be the main concern of researchers and in its place came the problems of population growth and distribution. Attempts were also made to establish population parameters and patterns of mortality and fertility for a variety of population groups with a view to getting a better idea of the situation in the country as a whole. The New Guinea Islands featured strongly in these works as well, for example, Epstein and Epstein (1962) give an account of the demographic situation in two Tolai villages and Scragg made follow-up studies of the population groups on Buka (1967) and an area near Kavieng (1968).

However, most of the studies cited above are based on very small sample sizes and some of the methods used are as questionable as are the results. In recent years though, certain researchers have used better methodologies and have collected adequate data or have utilised data from the census.

The recent work of Van de Kaa (1971) utilising the 1966 census and the administrative counts and reports from small areas estimated the crude birth rate to be 44 live births per 1,000 (mid-year population) and the crude death rate to be 22.4 per 1,000 (mid-year population). In addition, he estimated the total fertility rate to be 6.0; i.e. on average every woman bears six children in her childbearing years.

The research of Nou-Taboro (1978) is based on the 1971 census. The author utilised Brass's technique (see Chapter 6) to estimate childhood mortality and expectation of life for the country. The estimates were based on the proportion of children ever born who survived to the ages of 1, 2, 3, 5, 10, 15 and 20 from that reported as surviving to mothers in age ranges 15–19 to 45–49 years old; i.e. women in the childbearing age group. An attempt was made by the researcher to estimate infant mortality for males and females as well as rural and urban areas. Infant-mortality rates are provided for the various provinces and for the country as a whole. For the latter the rates are 137, 132 and 135 live births per 1,000 for males, females and both sexes respectively.

The work of Skeldon (1979) is based on the analysis of the 1971 population census of the three basic demographic variables (fertility, mortality and migration). The work updates the Van de Kaa findings with recent census data. Although the constraints of the data necessitated the use of different techniques, the results were very similar. Fertility is estimated to be high: the crude birth rate was between 44.7 and 46.0 per 1,000 in the population and the total fertility rate is in excess of 7.0 per woman. Mortality, on the other hand, has declined substantially from the 1966 level: the crude death rate is estimated to be 16.6 deaths per 1,000 in the population. Life-table death rates also reveal a considerable decline. Migration is primarily circular in that the majority of migrants return home, although there is a definite trend towards a more permanent population shift. The volume of migration is small by comparison with countries in other parts of the Third World.

In the area of family planning, a few researches are worth reviewing. Christie and Radford (1972) give an account of their attempt to provide family-planning services at the village level in the Kainantu subdistrict. They advanced four main points:

(1) A number of rural village people desire to either limit or space their children.
(2) The role of male attitudes may be very important in the success or otherwise of a family-planning programme for rural people.
(3) Villagers have misconceptions about modern family planning and this can be altered by frank discussions.
(4) Mobile village family-planning clinics can be established in Papua New Guinea.

Watson *et al.* (1973), assessing the acceptance of Lippes Loop and Depo-provera, concluded in an 'experience of 2000 women-months' of using the loop in the highlands that it is an acceptable form of contraception. They also reported that the use of Depo-provera at the family-planning clinic at the Port Moresby General Hospital over a period of 12 months proved to be an effective contraceptive acceptable to the majority.

Malcolm (1969) compared data from a family survey conducted in Lae with Bundi, a rural area in Madang Province. He found that Lae residents, especially permanent urban residents, tended to have shorter periods of breastfeeding, shorter intervals between births and larger families. The intervals increased with parity and traditional spacing was operating to some extent, especially among the migrant group who had steady intervals with a rise in parity. In these migrant families, the author found that there was an average spacing of two years and fertility was only restricted by a prolonged period of lactation. In Bundi, the birth intervals ranged between three and four years and were not related to parity. Families were smaller and breastfeeding lasted for three to five years and postpartum. A sex taboo also operated for most of this period.

Skeldon (1977) reported on family planning in the Goroka area of the Eastern Highlands and found that family planning was accepted by only 7 per-cent of the women in the childbearing age group. Given the high parity of the majority of acceptors and the high rejection rate of those nonacceptors of low parity, it can be seen that the family-planning programme has a long way to go before it can make a noticeable impact on the rate of population growth.

The research of Rafiq (1977, 1978) is the only one which investigates attitudes to knowledge of and the practice of contraception. The 1977 survey was carried out in selected areas of the Central and Northern Provinces. The results of this work show that the majority of the women in the sample were aware of both traditional as well as conventional methods of contraception. In addition, it was found that the majority of the respondents indicated that they would use contraceptives if the were easily acceptable. However, if potential future users are going to use contraceptives then it is safe to assume that the wife (and not the husband) would be the user. Further study is required into the attitudes of both males and females as to who should be the user. The 1978 study was carried out in the Kainantu area. Although a much more detailed survey, the results are similar to the previous one. The analysis of the ideal family size shows that the regulation of size is perceived to be more of an immediate problem for an urban family than for other types of family. The respondents seem to have a positive attitude towards the use of contraceptives. However, the proportion of 'everusers' was below the level when it could have a significant measurable impact on the overall level of fertility.

1.10 SPECIFIC AIMS OF THIS STUDY

On the whole, there is a lack of large-scale data on fertility, mortality and the use of contraceptives. Accordingly, this study focuses on these variables. Its primary objective is to provide information on vital rates (fertility, infant and child mortality) awareness, and knowledge of, attitudes towards and the practice of contraception among the population of Papua New Guinea which will provide the basis for the formulation and implementation of a population policy. Besides, the results may be used by the Department of Public Health for planning health services and improving existing ones as well as focusing on a target population in the area of family planning.

In addition, the study will establish a data resource bank which is urgently needed for development purposes. The survey also provided practical experience in the field for students in the Demography Unit of the Geography Department in the University of Papua New Guinea. It is also hoped that the study will make a significant contribution to our knowledge about fertility and infant- and child-mortality levels in the country, and about attitudes toward contraception, both conventional and traditional.

2

Methodology and Data Collection

2.1 RESEARCH SITES

The country was divided into four geographical regions for the purposes of data collection:

(1) New Guinea Mainland
(2) New Guinea Highlands
(3) New Guinea Islands
(4) Papua

The New Guinea Mainland is made up of four provinces namely: West Sepik, East Sepik, Madang and Morobe; the New Guinea Highlands consists of the provinces of Western Highlands, Southern Highlands, Chimbu, Enga and Eastern Highlands; the New Guinea Islands comprise Manus, East and West New Britain, New Ireland, and the North Solomons; and Papua consists of Western, Gulf, Northern and Milne Bay (see Figure 1).

For this phase of the study[1] data was collected from both urban and rural communities in each of the following geographical regions:

(1) New Guinea Mainland (East Sepik and Madang);

(2) New Guinea Highlands (Chimbu and Southern Highlands);

(3) New Guinea Islands (East New Britain and North Solomons);

(4) Papua (Milne Bay and Gulf).

Two provinces were selected from each of the four geographical regions for the

1. The funding organisations (Population Research Programme of Papua New Guinea) in cooperation with the Office of Environment and Conservation and the Department of Public Health Family-Planning Project) intend to support the data collection system from 1979 through to the end of 1982.

sample survey. The selection of provinces in each region was based on the needs of the Health Department as well as on logistic factors. For example, the Health Department needs information about how family-planning clinics and maternal and child-health clinics are being utilised, together with the current level of fertility and infant and child mortality. Besides noting the problems of transportation, the availability of interviewers and supervisors was also given serious consideration in selecting the provinces.

The provinces that were surveyed can be divided into two groups with regard to their physical and economic aspects. Milne Bay, Gulf, Southern Highlands and East Sepik have restrained economic growth because of a combination of historical and economic factors. Labour for the plantations was recruited on a large scale from these provinces in the past and, until recently, they were depleted of skilled labour and lacked economic development. Besides, the physical terrain of these provinces is inhibiting to large-scale agricultural development with swamps in Gulf and East Sepik, steep rugged mountains in Chimbu, Southern Highlands and Milne Bay and large expanses of water that are impassable in certain seasons.

East New Britain, the North Solomons and, to a lesser extent, Madang have established export-orientated agricultural industries based on a combination of largeholder and smallholder efforts. In East New Britain there are large-scale service industries for the copra industry in particular and, even though these industries are urban-based, their effects have spread to the surrounding rural areas. The North Solomons has the rich Bougainville Copper Mine which employs skilled labourers and has encouraged a conglomeration of service industries. The terrain in general in these three provinces is favourable to commercial agriculture.

2.2 SAMPLE DESIGN

A single-stage cluster-sample design was employed in the study for both the urban and rural areas. This design was adopted instead of a simple random-sample design because of the lack of household sampling frames and house addresses (especially in smaller urban and rural areas). Although some of the urban areas have household sampling frames, most of the urban communities in our sample did not. In addition, the lack of an efficient and dependable public transport system to facilitate movements between a large number of sample areas was a major problem. Besides, the funds made available for the research project were limited. Finally, it was beyond the scope of this survey to undertake the construction of sampling frames for the purposes of this study.

However, the 1971 census enumeration districts (CEDs), the available sampling frames and the village directory were used to assist in the selection of the cluster units,[2] 65 in all — 35 in the urban areas and 30 in the rural areas of the eight

---

2. A cluster as used in this survey is a group of households or villages.

provinces.[3] The selection of the clusters in the rural areas was based on both accessibility and the presence of clinics for maternal and child health and family planning. Once the sample communities were identified, the research officer visited the communities to make the initial contact with provincial officials and village 'big men' in order to lay down the groundwork for the impending survey. Attempts were also made during these visits to recruit as fieldworkers student nurses, health workers, teachers and, in some cases, high-school students (mainly those in the fifth and sixth forms) who were residents of the communities being surveyed. In addition, university students specialising in demography and those taking courses in demography were recruited as fieldworkers in some of the urban and rural communities. Supervisors were mainly health workers and teachers.

2.3 SAMPLE SIZE

The sample size of this phase of the survey was initially intended to consist of 1000 respondents in each province, except in the North Solomons where the survey was limited to the urban area of Kieta/Arawa/Panguna, where a sample size of 600 was adopted. The anticipated estimated sample size was 7,600 respondents — males and females regardless of their marital status. Two-thirds of the sample size consisted of females aged between 15 and 49 (i.e. of childbearing age) and one-third consisted of males aged between 20 and 54. The five-year differential between female and male cohorts reflects the tendency for women to form sexual unions with men a few years their senior. Both males and females who were living temporarily in the selected provinces were excluded as were those who had lived in these areas for less than six months.

The decision to sample more females than males was based on the primary aims of the survey. The estimated sample size of approximately 5,000 females of childbearing age was adopted because it was felt that it was large enough to provide reasonable data for the purposes of this survey. Similarly, the male sample size of 2,600 was considered to be adequate to yield sufficient data for the type of analysis that was intended. (See Data Collection and Analysis, 2.7.) Half of the sample was selected from urban communities and half from rural communities. This was because the data for each type of community needed to be analysed separately.

---

3. An urban area is defined as a town having a population of 5,000 or more. This definition is used to conform to recent Bureau of Statistics reports (1977 Urban Population Survey) and Agyei (1982a).

A rural area is defined as a traditional settlement with a population of less than 5,000 and lacks certain characteristics of urban areas such as established street patterns, contiguously aligned buildings and public services such as a piped water-supply, electricity, a police station, etc.

2.4 SELECTION OF THE RESPONDENTS

The criteria set out in the survey for the selection of the respondents were that the female respondents should be of childbearing age, between 15 and 49 years old and that the male respondents should be aged between 20 and 54. Either the wife or one of the wives of the head of the household[4] was selected. In the absence of the wife of the head of the household, any female of childbearing age was chosen. With regard to the male respondents, again the head of the household was selected but, in his absence, the oldest male aged between 20 and 54 was selected. In cases where the head of the household was female, any male whose age fell between the age limits set down for the survey was chosen.

One male was selected and interviewed for every two female respondents from different households in order to avoid the influence of the male opinions on the female and vice versa. Further, in order to minimise the influence of the opinions of one sex upon the other, female interviewers interviewed female respondents and male interviewers interviewed male respondents. Since only one respondent in each household[5] was interviewed, the number of respondents is equal to the number of households in the sample.

2.5 THE QUESTIONNAIRES

The data was collected by using questionnaires (male and female) which gathered information on three sets of variables — fertility, mortality (infant and child) and contraception. The questionnaires are reproduced in Appendix A. In general, the questionnaires were made up of about 85 per cent closed-ended and about 15 per cent open-ended questions. The open-ended questions were used to make an in-depth exploration into attitudes and perceptions of fertility behaviour and the use of contraceptives.

The female questionnaire consisted of 76 main items and sought information about the following general characteristics:

1. Personal characteristics: for example, age, education, marital status, religion, occupation, etc.
2. Household composition: (household membership chart).

---

4. The head of the household is the person who usually stays in the house and who owns the house or is responsible for the rent, or occupies the house by virtue of his employment. In cases where an arbitrary choice has to be made, the oldest male or the oldest female in an all-female household is considered to be the head.
5. A household is either a group of persons living in a dwelling who eat most meals together, are themselves responsible for organising all their own cooking, eating, toilet and other arrangements, or a person living alone in a dwelling who is responsible for organising all his or her own living arrangements.

3. Fertility data: (pregnancy record form) for each pregnancy, the age of the mother, the outcome of the pregnancy, prenatal and postnatal care, duration of lactation, age of each child at the time of the survey or at the time of death.
4. Data on living children: their place of residence, persons with whom they live, whether or not they attend school.
5. Mortality data: [6](infant and child) information on infant and child deaths during the twelve months preceding the survey and also deaths in the household other than those of infants and children during the twelve months preceding the survey.
6. Data on contraception: (conventional and traditional) the data collected is similar to that in the standard knowledge, attitudes and practice (KAP) surveys.
7. General data on children: family size, sex preference, perception of economic benefits from children, advantages and disadvantages of big and small families.

The male questionnaire consisted of 66 main items and sought information about six general characteristics:

1. Personal characteristics: for example, age, education, marital status, religion, occupation, etc.
2. Household composition: (Household membership chart).
3. Data on living children: their places of residence, persons with whom they live, and whether or not they attend school.
4. Mortality data: (infant and child) information on infant and child deaths during the twelve months preceding the survey, and also deaths occurring in the household other than infants and children during the twelve months preceding the survey.
5. Data on contraception: (conventional and traditional) the data collected are similar to those in the standard KAP surveys.
6. General data on children: family size, sex preference, perception, of economic benefits from children, advantages and disadvantages of big and small families.

The main difference between the male and the female questionnaires is that the female questionnaire included the pregnancy record form.

The questionnaires were drawn up in English, then translated into pidgin English with verification through an independent retranslation back into

---

6. It may not be possible to compute infant- and child-mortality rates directly from the sample. However, indirect techniques may be utilised where appropriate to estimate these rates.

English. The final versions of the questionnaires were drawn up in pidgin English and English.

A pretest was conducted before the actual collection of data. The pretest sample consisted of 53 respondents in urban and rural areas. The purpose of the pretest was to determine whether the items on the questionnaires were valid and reliable. This data was analysed for content with emphasis on the open-ended questions.

The length of the interviews ranged from about 45 minutes to two hours depending on the size of the family. However, on average, the interviews took about one hour to complete. The main problems encountered were disturbance by children, domestic activities and, rarely, the interference of the spouse.

2.6 ORGANISATION OF THE FIELDWORK

The nationwide nature of the survey (see Figure 1) made it necessary to set up fieldwork organisations in each of the provinces where the survey was conducted. Three supervisors were appointed (two for female interviewers and one for male interviewers) and in most cases the research officer and population educators from the Office of Environment and Conservation coordinated the survey in my absence. The supervisors distributed questionnaires to interviewers each morning and collected both completed and uncompleted questionnaires in the evening when the interviewers returned from the field. They also accompanied the interviewers into the field and carried out spot checks on the interviewers. In addition, they were responsible for verifying and editing one or more completed questionnaires from each interviewer from time to time to detect omissions and inconsistencies. The interviewers were also advised and helped by the supervisors when they encountered problems in the field.

On average, a total of 27 interviewers were employed in each province. Of the interviewers, 18 were female and 9 were male. The interviewers were employed full-time for the length of the survey which lasted approximately four weeks, including the training period. The interviewers and the supervisors were provided with an interviewer's manual (see Appendix B) and other materials, such as notable events list, maps, etc., prepared for the survey. They were then given basic training in interviewing techniques. The training involved:

1. Introduction to the survey;
2. Interviewing techniques;
3. Discussion and familiarisation with the questionnaires;
4. Practice interviews between interviewers;
5. Supervised practice interviews in the field which took place over about three to five days. The interviewers were aged between 18 and 35 with a mean age of about 22.

27

The fieldwork started in the middle of November 1979, included a break for Christmas and was completed in March 1980. The actual interviewing lasted for about three weeks in most of the provinces.

2.7 DATA COLLECTION AND ANALYSIS

The fieldwork covered eight urban centres, one in each province and 103 villages, which were divided into clusters based on the most recent population estimates (Bureau of Statistics, 1977, 1978). In the urban centres, council wards were used in forming 35 clusters and samples were taken from these. Since the survey required that only the indigenous population was eligible for interview, expatriate households in the clusters were excluded.

Most of the households were visited only once, although some were visited twice if no one was at home during the first visit. In some instances, an interviewer might be forced to discontinue an interview and continue at a subsequent visit. Such cases were few. Practically all the interviews were conducted at the homes of the respondents away from the rest of the family to ensure absolute privacy and confidentiality. The interviews were conducted in English and pidgin English except in Milne Bay and Gulf provinces where English and the local languages were used. The services of interpreters were used in Gulf Province to a limited extent.

Normally, the respondents were informed about the impending interview five to seven days beforehand, either by the local councillors or the health-extension officers. In addition, the local radio stations in the various provinces gave the survey a great deal of publicity by broadcasting its purpose in pidgin English and other local languages and also indicated where the interviewers would be from day to day. These periodic broadcasts came on the air in the mornings and evenings throughout the survey period in most of the provinces and were very helpful in getting a high response rate.

2.8 FIELDWORK RESULTS

This section deals briefly with results obtained in the field. Out of the 7,600 respondents anticipated, 6,391 were interviewed. This represents an 84 per cent response rate. Breaking these figures down into sex and place of residence, there was an 88 per cent response rate for the male sample (2,311 out of 2,600) and an 82 per cent response rate for the female sample (4,090 out of 5,000). The response rate from the rural areas was higher than that from the urban areas — 88 per cent (3,078 out of 3,500) and 81 per cent (3,323 out of 4,100) from the rural and urban areas respectively. The 16 per cent non-response rate was due to several reasons. Some of the prospective respondents were found to be ineligible for the study because of their age, whilst others were not at home and further efforts to contact them proved unsuccessful. Some prospective respondents simply refused to be interviewed.

The data collected formed the basis for the analysis of levels of fertility, mortality (infant and child) and attitudes towards family planning. The basis for the analysis of fertility and mortality is provided by the detailed histories of pregnancy on the female questionnaire (see Appendix A) in which all females in the childbearing group aged between 15 and 49 were questioned about the total history of their pregnancies, with many check questions to minimise omissions or inconsistencies in their reporting.

Several basic measures of fertility were estimated from the survey data. The first was age-specific fertility rates based on the births and age of mother. The second was the number of children born to women in the various age groups 15 to 19 years old to 44 to 49 years old. From the above measures of fertility, total fertility rates, gross reproduction rates and net reproduction rates were also estimated.

Data on the total number of children born and the children surviving to the females aged between 15 and 49 were used to estimate levels of infant and child mortality using some of the techniques developed by Brass *et al.* (1968); Brass (1975); Sullivan (1972); Feeney (1976); etc. The Brass and Sullivan techniques provide multipliers that are used to convert the proportion of the dead among the number of children ever born into more meaningful indices of infant and early child mortality. The Feeney technique also provides formulas that are easily utilised to compute infant-mortality levels and trends.

Finally, an intensive analysis was carried out of the data collected about the awareness, knowledge, attitudes and practice of contraception in terms of percentages according to sex, or whether the respondents lived in rural or urban areas, etc. Analysis was carried on some of the open-ended questions whenever appropriate.

2.9 DATA PROCESSING

The completed questionnaires were sent to the Demography Unit at the Geography Department of the University of Papua New Guinea. The data were edited and coded by a group of 20 students in accordance with the instructions set out in the coding manuals (male and female). Two-thirds of the coded sheets were keypunched onto computer tape by Computing for Commerce (PNG) Pty. Ltd., Port Moresby, Papua New Guinea and the remaining third was keypunched at the Department of Demography, Australian National University, Canberra, Australia. The computer tape prepared in Papua New Guinea was sent down to Canberra. Data cleaning was carried out by the author and Mrs Jennifer Widowson, computer programmer at the Department of Demography. The sample size was reduced to 6,283 respondents during the data-cleaning process as 108 cases were eliminated from the analysis for technical reasons. A

Table 2.1: Breakdown of data on fertility, mortality and contraception in Papua New Guinea

Provinces	Male respondents		Female respondents		Subtotal
	Urban	Rural	Urban	Rural	
1. Milne Bay	157	149	203	216	725
2. Gulf[a]	119	113	94	110	436
3. Chimbu	190	210	290	305	995
4. Southern Highlands	145	141	244	280	810
5. Madang	153	163	275	282	873
6. East Sepik	146	157	371	365	1039
7. East New Britain	138	133	311	299	881
8. North Solomons[b]	183	—	341	—	524
Subtotal	1231	1066	2129	1857	6283

Notes: a. Lack of female interviewers necessitated termination of survey.
      b. Survey was limited to urban areas of Kieta/Arawa/Panguna.

breakdown of the respondents by province, sex and residence is given in Table 2.1. The Statistical Packages for the Social Sciences (SPSS) were used in producing all the necessary tabulations for the analyses.

3

Some Socio-economic Characteristics of the Respondents and Selected Features of the Survey Population

3.1 SOCIO-ECONOMIC CHARACTERISTICS OF THE SAMPLE

A brief review of the social and economic characteristics of the sample population may be useful in the interpretation of the data and the results presented in Chapters 4 to 7. Tables 3.1A and 3.1B present data on five socio-economic characteristics ascertained in the survey for rural and urban respondents respectively. Literacy among the rural respondents is very low — 32.3 per cent of males and 36.5 per cent of females have no education; approximately 37 per cent of males and 42 per cent of females have had primary education. As expected, the urban respondents have an advantage over their rural counterparts in terms of education. Only 12.1 per cent of the urban males and 22.7 per cent of the females have no education. A third of the urban males sampled have had primary education. In terms of secondary and tertiary education, the urban males have an advantage over both the rural males and the urban females (see Table 3.1A and 3.1B).

The occupations in the rural areas are mainly agricultural. More than 50 per cent of both the male and female respondents in the rural areas are self-employed (including those owning stores or selling cash crops or involved with market sales). In the urban areas, only 4.6 per cent of the male respondents and 11.4 per cent of the female respondents are self-employed. The urban male respondents are involved either in the professions (10.3%), commerce (23.4%), clerical work (14.0%), manual work (including artisans; 24.2%) and in agricultural labour and domestic work (13.7%). It is important to note that while approximately 31 per cent of rural female respondents were unemployed at the time of the survey, approximately 62 per cent of the urban female respondents were unemployed (28.8 per cent were looking for employment and 33.1 per cent were not looking for employment).

Income levels tend to be low for both rural and urban respondents. About 31.3 per cent of the rural male and 29.1 per cent of the rural female respondents earn less than 50 kina per month. The percentages for the urban respondents who earn less than fifty kina per month are considerably lower (3.7 and 7.2 per

Table 3.1A: Selected social and economic characteristics among rural male and female respondents

Characteristics	Percentage distribution of respondents	
	Male	Female
Education		
No education	32.3	36.5
Primary	36.9	42.0
Secondary	9.7	5.3
Tertiary	5.6	2.1
Other	14.0	13.0
Omitted	1.5	1.0
Total	100	100
Occupation		
Self-employed (including trade store and PMV owners, cash crops and market sales	58.2	56.0
Professional	3.7	1.6
Commercial	3.9	2.0
Clerical	0.8	0.3
Manual trades (including artisans)	1.9	1.2
Labourers — general and agricultural (including domestics)	4.5	1.2
Unemployed	8.6	30.8
Other	4.0	0.4
Don't know	0.7	0.5
Omitted	13.7	6.0
Total	100	100
Monthly income		
No income	9.8	30.3
Less than K50	31.3	29.1
K50–K99	8.3	4.8
K100–K299	16.9	10.1
K300–K499	2.1	2.5
K500 and over	1.2	—
Don't know	1.4	1.3
Omitted	29.0	21.9
Total	100	100
Marital status		
Married	86.2	85.7
Divorced	1.9	2.8
Separated	1.8	1.4
Widowed	1.6	2.7
Single	8.5	7.4
Total	100	100
Age group		
15–19	2.0	8.7
20–24	23.2	17.5
25–29	20.5	18.8
30–34	16.3	17.7
35–39	13.7	15.9
40–44	10.1	10.4
45–49	7.5	7.9
50–54	5.7	—
Omitted	1.0	3.1
Total	100	100
Number sampled	1066	1857

Table 3.1B: Selected social and economic characteristics among urban male and female respondents

Characteristics	Percentage distribution of respondents	
	Male	Female
Education		
No education	12.1	22.7
Primary	33.3	45.4
Secondary	29.4	14.6
Tertiary	17.6	10.4
Other	6.4	6.0
Omitted	1.2	0.9
Total	100	100
Occupation		
Self-employed (including trade store and PMV owners, cash crops and market sales	4.6	11.4
Professional	10.3	9.5
Commercial	23.4	1.8
Clerical	14.0	5.3
Manual trades (including artisans)	24.2	0.6
Labourers — general and agricultural (including domestic)	13.8	—
Unemployed	1.5	61.9
Other	2.5	0.8
Don't know	0.7	0.1
Omitted	5.1	8.6
Total	100	100
Monthly income		
No income	2.0	63.6
Less than K50	3.7	7.2
K50–K99	8.0	3.2
K100–K299	72.9	13.7
K300–K499	4.4	0.4
K500 and over	0.9	0.2
Don't know	—	—
Omitted	8.0	11.5
Total	100	100
Marital status		
Married	84.2	92.7
Divorced	2.0	1.3
Separated	0.5	0.9
Widowed	0.1	0.5
Single	13.2	4.6
Total	100	100
Age group		
15–19	2.1	15.7
20–24	21.6	27.9
25–29	22.4	23.1
30–34	18.3	14.8
35–39	10.5	8.4
40–44	8.9	4.0
45–49	8.1	2.8
50–54	6.7	—
Omitted	1.4	3.4
Total	100	100
Number sampled	1231	2129

cent for male and female respondents respectively). The majority of the urban respondents earn between 100 and 299 kina per month (72.9 per cent of the male and 13.7 per cent of the female respondents). The figures for rural inhabitants in this category are 16.9 per cent male and 10.1 per cent female respondents respectively.

The data with regard to marital status show that the majority of respondents in both the rural and the urban areas were married. About 86 per cent of the rural male and female respondents were married, 84 per cent of the urban male and 93 per cent of the female respondents were also married. Divorce, separation and widowhood appear to be relatively rare (see Tables 3.1A and 3.1B). The proportions of single people among the rural respondents were 8.6 per cent and 7.4 per cent for male and female respondents respectively. The figures for the urban sample were 13.2 per cent for male respondents and 4.6 per cent for female respondents. The data show that 48.1 per cent of the rural male and 51 per cent of the urban male respondents were married between the ages of 20 and 24. Of the female respondents, 49.4 per cent of the rural female and 53.9 per cent of the urban female respondents were married between the ages of 15 and 19. The mean age for first marriage for the rural male and female respondents were 21.2 years and 17.4 years respectively, whilst the ages of their urban counterparts were 21.6 and 17.2 years respectively.

The urban male and female respondents in the age groups 20–24 and 15–19 (male and female respectively) have a slight edge over their rural counterparts in terms of early marriage. There are three possible explanations for this. Firstly, the sex ratio in the urban centres (Agyei, 1982) is significantly imbalanced in favour of males. Because of this, the demand for females is higher in urban areas and there is greater pressure on the urban females to marry at an earlier age than rural females. Secondly, common-law marriages are prevalent in the urban centres and there is a greater number of casual liaisons involving young men and women. Thirdly, unless a young woman has some kind of marketable skill, she becomes a burden in the urban area, and there is more pressure on her to marry to protect her reputation and, hopefully, to bring an income to her family through the payment of 'brideprice'.

A close examination of the age-distribution data of the responde.ts in Tables 3.1A and 3.1B reveals that the age distributions of the rural and the urban male respondents were similar. However, there is a striking difference in the age distributions of the rural and the urban female respondents. Approximately 45 per cent of the rural female respondents were under 30 years old and 52 per cent were aged 30 and over at the time of the survey. The corresponding figures for their urban counterparts were 67 per cent and 30 per cent respectively.

3.2 SELECTED FEATURES OF THE SURVEY POPULATION

3.2.1 The survey population

This section deals with some selected socio-economic characteristics of the total population covered by the survey. The entire population of the 65 cluster units — 35 in the urban areas and 30 in the rural areas — amounted to 43,575 including the 6,283 respondents (see Table 3.2). In terms of rural–urban breakdown, the rural population was 21,200 (10,327 males and 10,873 females) and the urban population was 22,375 (11,428 males and 10,947 females).

The literacy level of the population covered in the survey is low. From the data on years of schooling completed, substantial rural–urban and sex differences are evident. The data show that educational attainment was higher for both the rural and the urban males than for the rural and urban females. Approximately 49 per cent of the urban males and 35.6 per cent of the rural males indicated that they were literate. The figures for the urban and rural females are 30 per cent and 22.3 per cent respectively. The proportion of the population with no education generally rises with age for both the males and the females and the proportion with six or more years of schooling generally decreases, reflecting the trend towards higher education over the last decade or two.

Occupationally, the structure of the general population is similar to the sample. The majority of the rural population aged 15 years and above who were working at the time of the survey were involved in agricultural and related activities. Of the 86 per cent of the working males, 64 per cent were self-employed including farmers, 10 per cent worked in the professions, commerce and the clerical field and the remaining 12 per cent in manual work. Sixty-two per cent of the rural females were in market sales, 4 per cent in the professional, commercial and clerical categories and the remaining 27 per cent were self-employed.

The main differences evident in the data between the rural and the urban populations were that only a small proportion of the urban males and females were self-employed (7.4 per cent males and 15.8 per cent females). In addition, more rural females were employed than urban females. Seventy per cent of the urban females were not working at the time of the survey (37.2 per cent were not looking for employment and 22.8 per cent were looking for employment). The figures for the rural females was 38 per cent (21.4 per cent were not looking for employment and 16.6 per cent were looking for employment). About 50 per cent of the employed urban males were in the professional, commercial and clerical categories and the remaining 31.3 per cent were in manual trades, working as labourers, etc. — 11.3 per cent were unemployed.

The majority of the rural males and females earned less than 50 kina (K50.00) per month (45 per cent males and 51 per cent females). The figures for their urban counterparts in this income category were 8.6 and 15.1 per cent respectively.

Table 3.2: Distribution of the survey population by age and sex and sex ratio

| Age group | Rural | | | | Urban | | | | Sex ratio | |
| | Males | | Females | | Males | | Females | | | |
	Number	%	Number	%	Number	%	Number	%	Rural	Urban
0	279	2.7	218	2.0	238	2.1	259	2.4	128	92
1	257	2.5	242	2.2	273	2.4	255	2.3	106	107
2	366	3.5	421	3.9	471	4.1	459	4.2	87	103
3	342	3.3	378	3.5	427	3.7	447	4.1	90	96
4	408	4.0	459	4.2	477	4.2	452	4.1	88	105
0–4	1652	16.0	1718	15.8	1886	16.6	1872	17.1	96	101
5–9	1456	14.1	1479	13.6	1508	13.2	1565	14.3	98	96
10–14	1167	11.3	1272	11.7	1326	11.6	1226	11.2	92	108
15–19	940	9.1	1087	10.0	1120	9.8	985	9.0	86	113
20–24	971	9.4	913	8.4	983	8.6	1062	9.7	106	93
25–29	1002	9.7	935	8.6	1063	9.3	788	7.2	107	135
30–34	733	7.1	739	6.8	697	6.1	930	8.5	99	75
35–39	537	5.2	544	5.0	549	4.8	558	5.1	99	98
40–44	527	5.1	522	4.8	480	4.2	536	4.9	101	90
45–49	361	3.5	424	3.9	503	4.4	414	3.8	85	121
50–54	299	2.9	283	2.6	309	2.7	274	2.5	106	113
55–59	217	2.1	315	2.9	263	2.3	175	1.6	69	150
60–64	176	1.7	196	1.8	171	1.5	120	1.1	90	143
65+	114	1.1	217	2.0	274	2.4	153	1.4	53	179
Unknown	93	0.9	163	1.5	299	2.0	219	2.0	–	–
Omitted	83	0.8	66	0.6	67	0.6	68	0.6	–	–
Total	10,327	100.0	10.873	100.0	11,428	100.0	10.947	100.0	95	105

The majority of the urban males and females earned between 100 and 299 kina (K100.00–K299.00) per month. And the rural figures were 19 and 12.9 per cent for the males and the females respectively.

3.2.2 Age and sex structure of the survey population

Information on age and sex structure is always sought in all population censuses and surveys. Data on age and sex are important for both demographic analysis and other aspects of socio-economic planning programmes. The age and sex structure of a population at any time is the product of the combined effects of past trends in fertility, mortality and migration. In turn, the age and sex structure influences the current levels of fertility, mortality and migration rates. The age–sex structure of the population provides the basis for estimating the requirements for various essential goods and services and the data is also essential for population estimates and projections for the future.

Table 3.2 shows the percentage age–sex distribution of the survey population. The ages in the survey were obtained by asking for age in completed years, the year of birth and by reference to notable events in the lives of those whose ages were not known. The ages of about 58 per cent of the survey population were either given in completed years or year of birth by the respondents, 39.7 per cent were estimated by the interviewers from the list of notable events, and 2.3 per cent could not be estimated or were omitted. An examination of the number of males and females in the various age groups in Table 3.2 indicates that the age distribution suffered from misreporting. In addition, the excess of males over females in some of the age groups also indicates that the females were probably under-enumerated, particularly in some of the younger age groups. There is also some evidence of age heaping. The age distribution appears to be smooth for the younger age groups (0–4 to 15–19 years old). Fluctuations are evident in the age group 20–24 to 60–64 years old. These problems are not peculiar to Papua New Guinea. The age data in censuses and surveys is usually affected both by errors in the reporting of age and by variations in completeness of enumeration. The common causes of error in the developing countries are ignorance of age, deliberate misreporting or a misunderstanding of the question about age on the questionnaire.

A classification of the survey population into three broad age groups, namely 0–14, 15–64 and 65 and over shows that children under 15 constitute a large portion of the total population (42 per cent). The proportion aged between 15 and 64 represents 53.7 per cent, whilst the proportion of people aged 65 and over is a mere 2 per cent. The high proportion of children in the survey population is a direct influence of a high fertility level in Papua New Guinea.

Another measure of the youthfulness of a population is the median age i.e. the age at which half the population is above this age and half below. The median age for the survey population is 17.4 years. In 1966, the median age for Papua New Guinea was 19.1 and 17.6 in 1971. Evidently, a fall in the mortality rate, particularly among infants and children together with the control of infectious diseases accounts for this lower median-age level.

The age structure exhibited by the survey population with a heavy concentration of the population in the dependent age groups has both economic and demographic significance and implications. The economic significance lies in the relationship between age and economic activity and productivity. For the economy as a whole, the number of people gainfully employed is disproportionately small in relation to the unproductive groups who are dependent on them. This creates a burden for the economically productive population and is a hindrance to economic development.

An important aspect of a young and rapidly growing population is the problem of the burden of dependency. The dependency ratio is a simple statistical measure of the impact of age structure on the economic potential of a given population. It is assumed that the group aged between 15 and 64 years is the 'productive' segment of the population and that young people under 15 years old and those aged 65 and over are the 'dependent' segment. The dependency load that the productive population must bear is the ratio of the 'dependent' and 'productive' segments multiplied by 100. The ratio is a measure of the number of dependents that 100 people in the productive years must support. The dependency ratio computed from the data presented in Table 3.2 is 82 per cent. It must be pointed out that the true dependency ratio is probably higher because not all persons of working age are actually working.

The sex composition of a population is conveniently described by the sex ratio which is the most widely used measure of sex composition and is defined as the number of males per 100 females. A comparison of the sex ratios of the rural and urban areas (see Table 3.2) shows that the rural areas of Papua New Guinea have much lower ratios than the urban areas. The rural–urban migration of men in search of employment in the urban areas, which often necessitated leaving their families in their villages, is a well-known feature of life in Papua New Guinea and accounts for this problem. In a normal population not disturbed by migration, if the enumeration is accurate, or if the errors for males are as frequent and of the same magnitude as those for females, sex ratios will change gradually from one age group to another and the sex ratio will gradually decline with age (United Nations, 1956).

3.2.3 Proportion marrying and marital stability

The majority of ever-married men and women in the survey population were currently married at the time of the survey. The data presented in Table 3.3 indicate that approximately 83 per cent each of the rural males aged 20 and over and the females aged 15 and over were currently married. The proportion currently married among the urban population surveyed is similar to their rural counterparts. Of the urban males, 82 per cent aged 20 and over and 81 per cent of the urban females aged 15 and over were married. It is evident from the data presented in Table 3.3 that women marry at an earlier age than men. For example, in the 15–19 age group, 93.6 per cent of the rural males and 96 per cent of the urban males remained single compared with 44 per cent and 48 per cent of the rural and urban females respectively. This is also true for the group aged 20–24.

The instances of widowhood, divorce and separation also appear to be relatively small for the population surveyed. Widowed persons predominate in the older cohorts, especially those aged 45 and over. Widowhood ranges from less than one per cent for the age group 20–24 years to over 20 per cent for those aged 65 and above. The data reveal that widowhood is higher in the rural areas than in the urban areas. Higher mortality rates in the rural areas may account for the rural–urban differential in widowhood.

The number of divorce cases reported by the survey is rather small in each age group, ranging from 0.2 per cent to 1.8 per cent. The distributions of divorce cases for both the rural and urban populations are similar and indicate a high degree of marital stability. However, divorce and separation are sensitive

Table 3.3: Marital status of the survey population aged between 15 and 65 years old (percentages)

Age group	Rural						Urban					
	Never married		Currently married		Divorced		Never married		Currently married		Divorced	
	Males	Females	Males	Females	Males	Females	Males	Females	Males	Females	Males	Females
15–19	93.6	44.2	5.7	54.1	0.1	0.3	96.1	37.8	3.1	58.0	0.0	0.2
20–24	40.4	11.9	56.3	85.5	0.6	1.4	35.2	10.2	62.0	86.9	0.9	1.3
25–29	19.5	4.3	79.4	92.7	1.0	1.6	16.7	5.0	81.9	91.4	1.1	1.4
30–34	13.3	2.4	85.2	94.8	1.3	1.2	10.0	3.2	85.5	96.5	1.8	0.0
35–39	8.9	2.1	86.6	95.6	1.6	1.0	8.6	2.6	89.8	93.7	1.2	1.5
40–44	4.9	2.3	92.9	94.5	1.4	0.8	6.2	2.1	93.6	94.3	0.1	1.2
45–49	3.5	2.5	95.3	94.2	1.1	0.6	3.4	4.9	96.4	95.1	0.0	0.8
50–54	2.8	2.1	95.4	86.4	0.9	0.9	3.1	2.3	95.7	89.6	0.7	0.6
55–59	2.1	1.8	96.1	79.1	0.5	0.8	3.1	1.6	91.3	77.4	0.4	0.4
60–64	1.8	1.8	86.0	74.9	0.3	0.7	2.6	0.9	81.9	69.2	0.1	0.1
65+	2.2	1.6	72.2	68.2	0.7	1.2	4.8	2.0	75.3	74.5	0.3	0.5
Total	27.6	11.4	68.9	83.0			28.0	9.9	68.9	81.2		

areas of inquiry and some of the interviewers reported that respondents occasionally seemed reluctant to discuss their marital histories in detail. It seems likely therefore, that if there is an error in the data, it is likely that the proportions of divorce cases have been underestimated.

3.2.4 Household size

The word household is defined for the purpose of this survey as being either a group of persons living in a dwelling who eat most meals together, are themselves responsible for organising all their cooking, eating, toilet and other arrangements; or a person living alone in a dwelling who is responsible for organising all his/her own living arrangements. As we pointed out earlier under section 3.2.1., our analysis is based on 6,283 households within a total population of 43,575 (see Table 3.2).

Table 3.4 gives the distribution of households by the number of members. The mean size of household for the entire survey population is approximately seven persons per household and 7.3 and 6.6 persons per household for the rural and urban areas respectively. Morauta (1982) using the same definition reported similar figures for the rural and urban areas. What is evident in Table 3.4 is that the proportion of one-person households is very small and also that the majority of the households both in the rural and urban areas contains five or more people. Approximately 85 per cent and 78 per cent of the rural and urban households contained five or more members.

3.2.5 Household types

The data on household type give some information about the living arrangements of the sample population. In many rural areas of Papua New Guinea, especially in the Highlands areas, men and women live separately though their houses are on the same compound. In other areas, particularly in the coastal areas, men and women share the same dwelling, but in some instances have separate sleeping rooms — the men in one section of the house and the women and children in another. Alternatively, there is a communal sleeping area for family members of all ages and sexes.

Interestingly though, in the rural areas throughout Papua New Guinea, the husband and wife share a separate sleeping room away from the older members of the family, though they probably have one or two small children sleeping with them. In the urban areas, in the middle- and high-covenant housing areas, because of lack of space, all the members of the family share the same dwelling, but not usually the same sleeping room. These middle- and high-covenant houses are divided into rooms similar to the Western model — two or more rooms for sleeping, one for cooking, one for socialising, and a washroom. In low-covenant

Table 3.4: Distribution of households by number of members: Papua New Guinea

Number of members	Rural households		Urban households	
	Number	%	Number	%
1	29	1.0	82	2.4
2	114	3.9	212	6.3
3	178	6.1	171	5.1
4	155	5.3	282	8.4
5	222	7.6	413	12.3
6	228	7.8	655	19.5
7	468	16.0	507	15.1
8	459	15.7	390	11.6
9	588	20.1	403	12.0
10	368	12.6	91	2.7
11	44	1.5	60	1.8
12 or more	70	2.4	93	2.8
Total number of households	2923	100.0	3360	100.0
Total population	21200		22375	
Mean size of household	7.3		6.6	

housing areas and squatter settlements however, where there are houses of only one or two rooms, it is not uncommon for family members of all ages and sexes to sleep communally.

Table 3.5 shows that one-person households are not usual in Papua New Guinea, although the proportion appears to be slightly higher in the urban areas. The most common living arrangement both in the rural and urban areas is the

Table 3.5: Distribution of households by types: Papua New Guinea

Household type	Rural households		Urban households	
	Number	%	Number	%
Single person household	29	1.0	82	2.4
Husband — wife only	76	2.6	114	3.4
Husband — wife and children	849	29.0	1109	33.0
Husband — wife, children and others	1302	44.5	1653	49.2
Husband — wife, others, no children	489	16.7	337	10.0
Husband, more than one wife and children	35	1.2	17	0.5
Husband, more than one wife, children and others	33	1.1	10	0.3
Husband, more than one wife, others, no children	26	1.0	7	0.2
Other households	84	2.9	31	1.0
Total	2923	100.0	3360	100.0

husband, wife, children and others. This living arrangement is proportionately higher in the urban areas probably because of housing problems in these areas. The nuclear family comes second in both areas with the urban areas having higher numbers of such households than the rural areas.

A large proportion of the typical households of husband, wife, children and others are extended families, in which two or three generations live together and have a common living arrangement. The extended family is more common in the rural areas as 68.3 per cent of the rural households contain seven or more persons. The mean household size for the rural areas fits Bogue's (1969) expectations of a true extended family with a minimum of seven persons.

It is perhaps interesting to point out that polygamous or multi-wife households are relatively small compared with all other types of household in both the rural and urban areas. There are two possible explanations for this. One is the strong influence of Christianity throughout Papua New Guinea which advocates one wife. The other is that only a few men who are non-Christian can afford more than one wife in terms of the initial outlay of brideprice which has become somewhat inflated in recent times and of the sheer cost of keeping an extra wife or wives, especially in urban areas.

3.2.6 Relationship to head of household

Almost all the households in our survey had male heads except for about 2 per cent. This probably reveals that Papua New Guinea is a male-dominated society. The data presented in Table 3.6 show that the most common household residents in both the rural and urban areas, apart from the nuclear family, are other relatives. It is also evident that 20 per cent or more of the household residents were non-close relatives or non-relatives of the heads of the household. These

Table 3.6: Distribution of household members by relationship to head of household: Papua New Guinea

Relationship to head of household	Rural households		Urban households	
	Number	%	Number	%
Head	2923	13.8	3360	15.0
Spouse	2454	12.0	2998	13.4
Son or daughter	7335	34.6	6981	31.2
Son-in-law/daughter-in-law	2014	9.5	1544	6.9
Parent or parent-in-law	636	3.0	582	2.6
Brother, sister	572	2.7	1029	4.6
Grandchild	848	4.0	448	2.0
Other relative	3625	17.1	4318	19.3
Non-relative ('wantok')[a]	703	3.3	1115	5.0
Total	21200	100.0	22375	100.0

Note: a. 'Wantok' are people from the same cultural background, language group or even district.

figures are similar to Morauta's (1982) findings. The slightly higher percentage of 'other relatives' and non-relatives in the urban areas is related to the large proportion of 'other relatives' or 'wantoks' who are drawn to employment in the urban areas surveyed.

A comment should be made with regard to the high proportion of sons and daughters in the various households. The figures obtained for the female respondents in both the rural and urban areas were cross-checked with their surviving children and it was found that the rural and urban female respondents had 5.8 and 12 per cent more children 'em pikinini bilong mi' (i.e. he/she is my child), but who should in fact be categorised in other ways, especially if they live in the same household.

4

Breastfeeding and Sexual Abstinence[1]

4.1 INTRODUCTION

It is widely accepted that breastfeeding is universally used by the majority of mothers in the Third-World countries. Today, increasing concern about maternal and child health in the Third-World countries has focused attention on the multiple advantages of breastfeeding and its impact on health, nutrition and fertility. However, the practice of breastfeeding is declining in some of the urban areas of many Third-World countries. This decline has been caused by vigorous commercial promotion of milk formulas and food supplements for infants, by changing the perception of the acceptability and social status of breastfeeding and to a lesser extent, by increasing employment of women outside the home where no provision is made for breastfeeding.

Breastfeeding is extensively used and socially sanctioned in Papua New Guinea. It is also promoted by the government (Health Department) for its hygienic nutritional value to the infant. The government's programme was initiated in 1977 to reduce the level of infant mortality by banning indiscriminate bottle-feeding which was causing an increase in the number of infant deaths because of lack of hygiene and heavily diluted artificial feeding formulas. The programme did not consider breastfeeding as a method of family planning. The practice of breastfeeding and sexual abstinence in Papua New Guinea does not vary markedly between the urban and rural areas and has not been significantly changed by the introduction of modern contraceptive methods.

4.2 BREASTFEEDING

Sexual abstinence is practised by many couples in both the rural and urban areas of Papua New Guinea while the woman is breastfeeding to prolong the period

1. A condensed form of this chapter has been published in the Journal of Biosocial Science. Vol. 16 No. 4, 1984, and it is reproduced here (with some additional material) with the kind permission of the Galton Foundation.

of breastfeeding for nutritional purposes and in accordance with traditional beliefs. In this section the differential patterns of breastfeeding in terms of place of residence, educational level and socio-economic status, place of birth of urban respondents and place of delivery of the babies will be examined. These differentials will give a better understanding of the status of breastfeeding in Papua New Guinea.

4.2.1 Place of residence

The data reveal that there is scarcely any significant difference in the attitude of the rural and urban respondents towards breastfeeding. Table 4.1 indicates that more than 90 per cent of the rural and urban male respondents believe that breastfeeding provides good food for children. In answering the question 'Why do you believe in breastfeeding?' approximately 55 per cent of the rural male respondents said 'breast milk is better food for the children' and another 22 per cent said 'breast milk is natural food for children'. The figures for their urban counterparts are approximately 52 per cent and 20 per cent respectively. The respondents were asked whether all their children were breastfed. Responses show that 81.1 per cent of the rural males and 85.6 per cent of the rural females indicated that their children were all breastfed. Unlike the rural respondents, there is a wide difference between the answers supplied by males (72.3 per cent) and the urban females (87.2 per cent). Since the answers are based on retrospective recollection of events, there is a great likelihood of misreporting.

Table 4.1: Percentage of rural and urban male and female respondents answering selected questions on breastfeeding: Papua New Guinea

Respondents	Belief in breast-feeding	Better food for children	Natural food for children	All children breastfed	Period of breast-feeding (mean number of months)
			Rural		
Male	93.1	54.9	21.8	81.1	—
Female	—	—	—	85.6	21.8
			Urban		
Male	92.1	51.5	20.0	72.3	—
Female	—	—	—	87.2	20.7

The period of breastfeeding ranged from 3 to 48 months for the last surviving child, with only 9.2 per cent of rural and 6.6 per cent of urban mothers breastfeeding for less than 15 months. Only 2.1 per cent of the rural mothers and 1.6 per cent of the urban mothers breastfed for a period up to 48 months.

45

The mean period of breastfeeding for the rural mothers is 21.8 months and that for the urban mother is 20.7 months. On the whole, the data presented in Table 4.1 reveals very little difference between rural and urban areas in terms of breastfeeding practices.

Dow (1977) notes that there is growing evidence that variations in the duration of breastfeeding reflect national responses to health conditions. In Papua New Guinea, health services vary from province to province but some are generally below average, particularly in rural areas. However, the government of Papua New Guinea has had a successful programme promoting breastfeeding since 1977 (see Baer, 1981 for details). Dow (1977) notes further that richer urban women are able to compensate for the benefits of prolonged breastfeeding because of their greater access to modern amenities — as far as nutritional alternatives for their infants are concerned. The slightly lower mean duration of breastfeeding for urban female respondents in Table 4.1 complies with Dow's assertion.

4.2.2 Educational level and socio-economic status

The educational level and socio-economic status of the respondents is important with regard to attitudes toward breastfeeding. As discussed earlier, the literacy levels of both the rural and the urban respondents are rather low (see Tables 3.1A and 3.1B). These tables indicate that a higher percentage of the urban female respondents have been educated to secondary level than their rural counterparts (14.6% and 5.3% respectively). This, together with their greater accessibility to facilities, accounts for the lower mean duration of breastfeeding reported for the urban female respondents in Table 4.1. On the other hand, the low standard of education in many urban female respondents is a major factor in explaining why their mean period of breastfeeding is not significantly different from their rural counterparts, even though the urban female respondents have greater access to facilities.

Jain and Bongaarts (1981) note that the husbands' occupation seems to have a consistent independent effect on the breastfeeding behaviour of the women in the eight developing countries which they surveyed. In Papua New Guinea, however, the programme to promote breastfeeding has counteracted whatever effect this may have had. Instead, the occupation of women, as already mentioned, would seem to be the regulator of the breastfeeding behaviour of Papua New Guinean women. The husband's and/or the father's attitude (pertaining to his acquired or aspiring socio-economic status) would only have an effect on breastfeeding insofar as he influenced his wage-earning wife/daughter to return to work shortly after giving birth. (There is no evidence of this.)

4.2.3 Place of birth of urban respondents

Knodel and Debavalya (1980) suggest that urban women born in rural areas breastfeed more extensively than native urban women. Indeed, historical economic trends in Papua New Guinea have activated a great deal of inter-provincial migration and have caused an unbalanced pattern of economic development in the country.[2] This unbalanced development has been the indirect cause of recent migration from the old labour-recruiting areas to the large urban centres. This rural–urban movement has also been accelerated by the expansion of the education system which, in the main, trains people for urban-based employment, and has been facilitated by air and road links to major centres.

Table 4.2: Percentage distribution of urban respondents born in urban areas: Papua New Guinea

Province of interview	% of respondents				% born in urban areas			
	Male		Female		Male		Female	
East New Britain	11.2	(138)[a]	14,7	(311)	5.5	(68)	8.1	(172)
East Sepik	11.9	(146)	17.4	(371)	8.6	(106)	16.4	(349)
Gulf	9.7	(119)	4.4	(94)	5.8	(72)	3.1	(67)
Madang	12.4	(153)	12.9	(275)	9.4	(116)	7.5	(161)
Milne Bay	12.8	(157)	9.5	(203)	10.5	(129)	9.6	(204)
North Solomons	14.8	(183)	16.0	(341)	6.6	(81)	6.5	(139)
Chimbu	15.4	(190)	13.6	(290)	11.0	(135)	10.5	(225)
Southern Highlands	11.8	(145)	11.5	(244)	8.7	(107)	9.6	(206)
Not applicable	—		—		33.9	(417)[b]	28.7	(606)[b]
Total	100.0	(1231)	100.0	(2129)	100.0	(1231)	100.0	(2129)

Notes: a. Figures in parentheses represent number of respondents.
b. Number of respondents born in rural areas.

Table 4.2 gives some idea of current rural–urban migration patterns in Papua New Guinea and this mobility of people is instrumental in perpetuating patterns of breastfeeding behaviour in the rural–urban settings. Table 4.2 shows that 33.9 per cent of the male respondents and 28.7 per cent of the female respondents in the urban areas were born in rural areas. The data reveal that the mean duration of breastfeeding for the rural-born urban-resident mothers is 21.4 months and that for the native urban mothers is 20.3 months. Even though the difference is comparatively small, it is interesting to note that rural-born

2. That is the plantation industry and its large-scale recruitment of labour from East Sepik, Highlands, Gulf and other provinces to the plantation-concentrated areas of Gazelle Peninsula, New Ireland, the North Solomons, East Papua Mainland and to a lesser extent, Madang.

urban-resident mothers breastfeed for a slightly shorter time than rural mothers (21.4 and 21.8 months respectively).

The tendency for ethnic groups to 'stick together' in new environments is a major contributing factor to the persistence of old ideas which are socially acceptable within a particular group. Therefore, although the urban setting probably '. . . fosters the reduction of breastfeeding' according to Knodel and Debavalya (1980) by offering alternatives, this must be offset against popular traditional practices like breastfeeding, the practice of which is being reinforced by government policy.

4.2.4 Place of delivery

An increasing number of Papua New Guinean women are having their babies in hospitals (see Table 4.3). This contact with modern health facilities allows the women a greater awareness of the alternatives available to long periods of breastfeeding.

Table 4.3: Percentage distribution of births to rural and urban female respondents by place of delivery: Papua New Guinea

Place of delivery	Percentage of births	
	Rural	Urban
Village	53.1	19.5
Clinic	2.8	2.3
Hospital	40.3	73.9
Aid post	0.5	0.7
Omitted	3.3	3.6
Total	100.0	100.0
Number of live births	8074	5809
Number of respondents with children	1629	1839

Knodel and Debavalya (1980) report (with regard to their Thai data) that exposure to certain negative attitudes amongst hospital staff and certain procedures in maternity hospitals tends to unconsciously encourage bottlefeeding. However, as we pointed out earlier, breastfeeding has been actively promoted in Papua New Guinea since 1977, especially in maternity wards, because of its hygienic and nutritional value to the infant. In fact, the promotion of breastfeeding as a reliable infant food has been instrumental in reducing the level of infant deaths in both the rural and urban areas. Biddulph (1980) utilising scanty data from the Port Moresby General Hospital shows that there has been a significant increase in breastfeeding from 65 per cent in 1975/76 to 88 per cent in 1979. He further shows that the deaths of infants under 6 months from gastroenteritis has been reduced from 30 per cent of those admitted in 1975 to nil in 1978/79. According to Biddulph (1980), babies under six months old have been singled out as milk is the main diet for this age group. Hence changes in numbers of infants suffering from gastroenteritis in this age group are likely to reflect changes in feeding practices.

Although other infant feeding alternatives are available at the place of delivery, their use is generally limited to only a few mothers who for one reason or another cannot breastfeed.

4.3 SEXUAL ABSTINENCE

The practice of sexual abstinence in Papua New Guinea is institutionalised and very common in many societies in the country according to Bulmer (1971) and is a result of the existence of various taboos that limit sexual activity among couples. As already mentioned, couples are supposed to refrain from sexual activity while a child is breastfeeding. In certain societies, the men abstain during the season when the crops are sown (e.g. the Trobians of Milne Bay) and also during the harvest. Both men and women abstain when they have to perform certain traditional rituals or ceremonial activities.

Again we shall attempt to examine sexual abstinence in terms of the place of residence, age at first marriage and communication between spouses, other family members and institutions. It will be evident that the amount of social change that has occurred in Papua New Guinea has not had a significant adverse effect on the practice of sexual abstinence.

The respondents were asked if they thought that a man and his wife should go without sexual relations after a child is born and how long should this time be (questions 34 and 34a and 42 and 42a on the male and female questionnaires respectively). The responses and the mean duration of sexual abstinence are presented in Table 4.4. About 63 per cent of the rural male and 67 per cent of the female respondents responded positively, and approximately 34 per cent of the rural male and 29 per cent of the female respondents answered negatively. The figures for the urban male and female respondents responding affirmatively are 66 per cent and 74 per cent respectively; and for those responding negatively, 31 per cent and 22 per cent male and female respectively.

The duration of sexual abstinence ranges from one month to 36 months with only a few respondents abstaining for a longer period. The main reason for postpartum abstinence is consideration for the welfare of the child — waiting 'until the child is big enough'. The mean duration of sexual abstinence for the rural male respondent is 21.4 months and that for the female respondents is 20.2 months. The figures for their urban counterparts are 19.5 months and 16.6 months respectively (see Table 4.4).

Table 4.4: Percentage of rural–urban male and female respondents answering selected questions about sexual abstinence: Papua New Guinea

Respondents	Yes	No	Omitted and don't know	Period of sexual abstinence (mean number of months)
		Rural		
Male	62.8	33.7	3.5	21.4
Female	66.7	29.3	4.0	20.2
		Urban		
Male	66.0	30.5	3.5	19.5
Female	73.9	21.7	4.4	16.6

4.3.1 Place of residence

The place of residence has an important influence on the amount and type of social experience an individual is exposed to and helps to explain the continuance or disintegration of cultural values which, in many instances, revolve around a particular work routine. In Papua New Guinea, the place of residence does not affect the practice of sexual abstinence, although its practice in the urban areas is governed to a lesser extent by sexual taboos. In both the rural and urban areas, sexual abstinence is highly regarded and in many instances, postpartum abstinence is deemed essential for the welfare of the child (about 80 per cent of both rural and urban respondents advocating postpartum sexual abstinence).

Bulmer (1971) gives a comprehensive account of what he terms 'institutionalised restrictions on cohabitation in Papua New Guinea'. He says the most notable of these are limitations enforced in the early period of marriage, postpartum sex taboos and taboos associated with male rituals or ceremonial activities.

With regard to enforced limitations on sexual relations in the early period of marriage, the data in this report indicate that although a large proportion of both rural and urban female respondents first marry between the ages of 15 and 19 (49.4 per cent and 53.9 per cent of the rural and the urban female respondents respectively) many do not begin childbearing until they are aged between 20 and 24. This tends to confirm Bulmer's account of the practice of sexual limitations in the early period of marriage, especially in the rural areas, where traditions and the women's work routine have not been influenced by modernisation as in the urban areas. It is also evident from the data that women in rural areas marry at the same time as their urban counterparts (the mean age for first marriages for rural and urban women are 17.4 and 17.2 years respectively) but begin their childbearing later (the mean age for childbearing for rural and urban women are 26.4 and 24.0 years respectively) than urban women. This could be due to a combination of belief in sexual abstinence during the early stages of marriage, their work routine, a greater involvement in ceremonial activities and the fact that their husbands may work long distances away from home in other provinces for extended periods of time. The urban women begin childbearing earlier because a large proportion of them (61.9 per cent) are not working (see Table 3.1B). In these circumstances there is no pressing work routine for the women and it is easier for them to have children. It therefore seems that urban couples do not feel such a great need to practise sexual abstinence for such an extended period in the early stages of marriage as do rural couples.

4.3.2 Age at first marriage

The age when the first marriage takes place helps to assess the amount and type of information that has accumulated through formal education and life experience before marriage. Van de Kaa (1971) suggests that '. . . the least educated section of the population may not be sufficiently motivated to use modern contraceptives for sustained periods'. As already mentioned, the level of education of the respondents in the survey, especially the women in both the rural and the urban areas of Papua New Guinea, is low. Coupled with this, the youthfulness of the females at first marriage (aged between 15 and 19) is significant (49.4 per cent in rural areas and 53.9 per cent in urban areas) because this is a highly impressionable age — one in which they are easily influenced by the norms of their peer group. Papua New Guinean society remains conservative and generally a young person's peers are found within their family and ethnic groups if they are not exposed to outside influence through higher education.

The data also show that a large proportion of the males are not much older than the females when they get married (48 per cent of rural males and 51 per cent of urban males marry between the ages of 20 and 24) and for many, their social experience before marriage would not be much more than that of their wives. This lack of social experience of both husband and wife and also the lack of education could greatly inhibit communication between spouses, especially with regard to contraception (see Table 4.5), and would also allow them little resistance to family pressure to comply with traditional norms and social sanctions surrounding the procreation of children.

It would appear, then, that the age of couples at first marriage in Papua New Guinea has a direct influence on the extent to which they stick to traditional norms and their attitudes with regard to the serious use of alternatives to sexual abstinence.

4.3.3 Household communication

Most Papua New Guineans in both rural and urban areas live in an extended-

Table 4.5: Percentage distribution of communication with regard to contraceptives between spouses of rural and urban male and female respondents: Papua New Guinea

Communication	Males	Females
Rural		
Possible	21.7	27.5
Actual	16.7	20.3
None	29.0	26.4
Not applicable	13.8	14.3
No response	16.5	7.5
Omitted	2.3	4.0
Total	100.0	100.0
Number of cases	1066	1857
Urban		
Possible	29.1	35.3
Actual	23.1	28.9
None	20.0	17.7
Not applicable	15.8	7.3
No response	8.4	7.1
Omitted	3.6	3.7
Total	100.0	100.0
Number of cases	1231	2129

family system. With regard to sexual abstinence, it is necessary to look at communication between adult members of such a family structure as well as that between the spouses. However, information on communication other than that between the spouses is scanty and difficult to gauge from this survey.

It would appear, then, that both the household and the community could have a great deal to do with the amount of communication between husbands and wives. In the rural areas, the small-scale community has a real effect on urging conformity with traditional norms. In the urban areas, where the extended family structure fulfils the role, its impact on a couple is governed by the socio-economic status of the husband or father or whoever is head of the household. Also, the constant presence of other adults and older children could have a significant inhibiting effect on discussions between spouses, especially anything related to contraception. These factors could have the effect of counteracting accessibility to family-planning services, especially in urban areas, and may indirectly perpetuate the use of sexual abstinence.

Table 4.5 gives some indication of communication between spouses. Although the possibility for communication is between 21.7 and 27.5 per cent for rural male and female respondents, actual communication is only possible between 16.7 and 20.3 per cent of the rural male and female respondents. The corresponding figures for the urban respondents are between 29.1 and 35.3 per cent possible communication and between 23.1 and 28.9 per cent actual communication for male and female respondents respectively. The most common reason for lack of communication where it is in fact possible has been recorded in the questionnaires as 'other' for all respondents. It may be assumed that a large proportion of 'other' could be because of lack of privacy in the home.

4.3.4 Institutional communication

The media and the interaction with various institutions which expound modern information is a significant factor in spreading information about alternatives to traditional practices and beliefs, such as sexual abstinence. However, the data indicate that the impact of contact with the institutions on users and non-users of contraceptives in Papua New Guinea is very slight indeed. People with lower incomes, for instance, may not have a radio. There are various advertisements and comic strips encouraging community-based distribution of condoms in the major newspapers but many people may not have the inclination to read the newspaper other than the sports page and others cannot read.

In Papua New Guinea, the hospital or clinic is the place where most users and non-users acquire information about family planning. Information from relatives is the second most common source (see Table 7.4 in Chapter 7) and this could be related to the amount of influence that adult members of the family have over the practice of contraception. That is, the husband or wife may feel obliged to use or not to use a particular method if so advised by an older and/or respected member of the family.

Men usually head the power structure within the household, and the husband's or father's institutional communication can have a great deal of impact upon the decision he or his wife or daughter makes with regard to traditional versus modern forms of contraception. It is necessary for husbands to sign a consent form before the wife can be issued with a modern contraceptive from the family-planning clinic. Contraceptives are not issued to single women. Since the educational and socio-economic levels of the majority of the male respondents are low, the negative attitude toward modern contraceptives may be due to lack of higher formal education and the monetary factor (the cost of Depo-provera for example, is K5 or 7 US dollars). These factors may indirectly restrict couples to the use of sexual abstinence.

The main problem with regard to institutional communication, particularly in the ritual areas, is that health-extension workers or aid-post orderlies are virtually all men. These workers may not feel confident, or may be discouraged by the community from communicating directly with women about contraception and vice versa, and the rural men may be too conservative or too embarrassed to approach the health-extension worker or aid-post orderly, who is usually a stranger in the community.

Sexual abstinence is being indirectly promoted by the government's breastfeeding programme introduced in 1977. The programme has consolidated the traditional practice of sexual abstinence which accompanies breastfeeding in Papua New Guinea as an automatic social phenomenon, and hence, its use as a contraceptive method is also consolidated.

4.3.5 Taboos surrounding breastfeeding and sexual abstinence

The majority of the male and female respondents in both the rural and urban areas feel that it is 'bad to have sexual relations while a woman is breastfeeding a child'. The taboos surrounding this feeling are the adverse effects sexual relations will have on the current child. According to Bulmer (1971) some of the adverse effects include poisoning breast milk, illness, abnormal growth and even death. There is a traditional belief that the semen from the man actually enters and poisons the breast milk which is being fed to the baby. Singarimbum and Manning (1976) reported that the rural females of Mojolama in Central Java believe that the detrimental effect of sexual relations on a nursing mother's milk is caused by the entry of the semen into the womb. Caldwell and Caldwell (1977) also reported similar popular beliefs among the Yoruba of Nigeria. Such a popular belief among Papua New Guineans which discourages a nursing mother from having sexual relations with her husband show that breastfeeding and sexual abstinence are closely linked in the Papuan New Guinean society. Caldwell and Caldwell (1977) also discovered from their Nigerian data that the duration of breastfeeding and sexual abstinence are related. Singarimbum and Manning (1976) also reported that the practice of sexual abstinence is indeed closely related to breastfeeding. In Papua New Guinea, the data from the rural areas tends to give some support to the relationship between sexual abstinence and breastfeeding. The mean duration of sexual abstinence for the rural female respondents was 20.2 months, (see Table 4.4) and the mean duration of breastfeeding was 21.8 months (see Table 4.1).

The urban data appear to be influenced by the younger female respondents (i.e. those under 30 years old) who have completed secondary education or gone beyond secondary school. This group has a slightly shorter mean duration of sexual abstinence (14.3 months). While it appears from the data that the norms of breastfeeding and sexual abstinence of Papua New Guinean women, namely, the rural and less well-educated have remained almost intact, there is a possible trend towards a relatively shorter period of sexual abstinence among the urban and the relatively well-educated. As these latter groups tend to be social innovators whose habits are followed in due course by others, this finding is disturbing as it may influence breastfeeding in the long run. Since it is not acceptable for a nursing mother to be pregnant, women would tend to abruptly suspend breastfeeding as soon as they recognise a new pregnancy. Cantrelle and Leridon (1971) have suggested that a child's chances of survival tend to diminish when a new pregnancy has forced an early weaning of the last-born child.

Although the data indicate that the majority of Papua New Guinean women are not aware of the fertility-limiting effects of breastfeeding, it is the opinion of the author that breastfeeding may have a significant role in limiting fertility, both by delaying the resumption of ovulation after childbirth and by its association in Papua New Guinean society with sexual abstinence.

4.4 SUMMARY AND CONCLUSION

It is evident from our recent survey that the most important determinants of the use of breastfeeding and sexual abstinence in Papua New Guinea are:

(1) Place of residence, relating more to a woman's work routine rather than to accessibility or non-accessibility to services;
(2) the educational and socio-economic levels of respondents and that of the husbands of female respondents;
(3) place of birth of urban respondents;
(4) place of delivery;
(5) age at first marriage;
(6) communication — household and institutional.

In consideration to these factors, it must be emphasised that the two major urban centres in Papua New Guinea, Port Moresby and Lae were not included in the survey.[3] This, and the fact that most of the rural areas surveyed have reasonable access to urban centres could account for the similarity in the rural and urban results. Other factors which could account for this similarity are the low education and socio-economic levels both in the rural and the urban areas and the relatively large proportion of 'rural-born' urban residents.

The Papua New Guinean government has successfully promoted breastfeeding as it considers breast milk to be a hygienic, reliable and nutritious infant food. This action has done much not only to reduce the level of infant deaths, but also to consolidate the practice of sexual abstinence which is the culturally acceptable behaviour while breastfeeding both in the rural and the urban areas.

The hospital is increasingly becoming the most common place of delivery in Papua New Guinea and this has had a very positive effect on the promotion of breastfeeding in the country. Exposure to its facilities is gradually having an impact on the methods of child-spacing used in the urban areas, but the use of modern methods is not taken seriously as indicated in the Knowledge, Attitude

---

3. Thomas McDevitt in his project 'Family and Fertility in Port Moresby' collected similar information on 118 men and 94 women in Port Moresby and thus Port Moresby has been omitted in this survey. However, the author of this report carried out a similar survey in Lae between June and July 1981. (This survey will be reported separately.)

and Practice (KAP) section of our survey, reported in Chapter 7, which deals with family size and family planning.

The age at first marriage, especially that of the women, seems to have some relationship with the practice of breastfeeding and sexual abstinence in as much as it relates to the amount of formal education and social experience the woman has had before marriage and her susceptibility to family pressure with regard to conformity within cultural norms.

A large number of women in Papua New Guinea do not appear to be aware of the inhibiting effect of breastfeeding and sexual abstinence on fertility. The main reason for prolonged breastfeeding and sexual abstinence is to ensure the welfare of the mother and child (which is indirectly, a means of child-spacing). Data derived from the KAP portion of this survey indicate that 23.5 and 16.5 per cent of the rural female respondents were using breastfeeding and sexual abstinence respectively as methods of child spacing. The corresponding figures for their urban counterparts are 16.4 and 12.9 per cent for breastfeeding and sexual abstinence respectively.

The data relating to breastfeeding and sexual abstinence reflect the practices of a society that places great value on having large numbers of children. Evidently, the only factors checking natural fertility are the cultural factors limiting family size within marriage such as the sexual limitations enforced in the early stages of marriage, postpartum sex taboos and taboos associated with male ritual or ceremonial activities. In addition, the incidence of polygamy and marital instability may also serve to limit natural fertility.

5

Fertility Levels, Patterns and Differentials

5.1 INTRODUCTION

Fertility is a complex demographic process responsible for the maintenance of society. The fertility behaviour of a given population is influenced by a number of complicated factors which are not well-defined, hence the difficulty in constructing an appropriate model for fertility analysis. In spite of these problems, various studies have placed emphasis on the role of demographic, socio-economic and cultural variables in determining differences in fertility behaviour between and within populations (Davis and Blake, 1956; Bongaarts, 1978). Nevertheless, the link between these variables and fertility is not clear-cut because of the effects of further intermediate variables. For example, education may affect fertility by delaying the age of marriage or by making women aware of contraception. In this example, the main variables affecting fertility are the age at which marriage takes place and the use of contraceptives and not education *per se*. Similar explanations may be given for the relationship between fertility and rural–urban residence, etc.

Estimates of fertility levels, patterns and differentials for Papua New Guinea have been based on data from the 1966 and 1971 censuses because of the lack of data giving vital statistics. The data from the censuses have various inherent problems (Agyei, 1982b) and, as such, the estimates of fertility levels, patterns and differentials do not give the true picture of fertility as the data are not adjusted before being used. The analysis of fertility levels, patterns and differentials in this chapter are based on a sample survey in which the following information was collected: (1) births occurring in the twelve months preceding the survey; (2) the recorded retrospective fertility (number of children ever born) of all the female respondents; (3) a complete history of the pregnancies of all the female respondents; (4) the age structure of the female respondents.

The questions on the histories of pregnancy obtained the birth date of each child or an estimated age and also the date of each pregnancy that did not result in a live birth. The age of children not currently living was also recorded. It is usually claimed that, while such data provide a useful measure of fertility, they tend to underestimate the true levels of fertility. This underestimation is the result of the tendency of women to forget the births of children who died in the first year of life. It is further claimed that data concerning the history of pregnancy tend to produce an artificial decline in period fertility rates because of an overestimation of fertility in the recent past. This is due to misstatements about the ages of children by older women ('recall lapse'). These errors can be minimised by the careful training of the interviewers in the techniques of probing when collecting data about life histories, as was the case in this survey.

This chapter focuses attention on the current and cumulative fertility of the respondents and an attempt is made to examine fertility differentials in terms of rural–urban dwelling, geographical (regional) situation and the level of education. Education is selected in preference to other socio-economic variables because it is largely unchanging during the course of the childbearing years.

5.2 CURRENT FERTILITY

This section includes an examination of the pattern and level of current fertility; i.e. fertility in the twelve-month period preceding the survey. This information is perhaps most important and relevant for planning and policy-making because of its impact on current and future population growth. Three measures of current fertility will be presented in this section: the crude birth rate (CBR), age-specific fertility rates (ASFR) and total fertility rates (TFR).

5.2.1 The crude birth rate

The crude birth rate, which is related to the total population regardless of variations in age and sex is a rough measure of fertility level. Data on the number of children aged one year old and under and the enumerated populations (rural and urban) of the survey areas form the basis for the estimation of the crude birth rate (see Table 3.2). The estimates of the crude birth rates are given in Table 5.1 together with estimates from the censuses of 1966, 1971 and 1980. The levels of the crude birth rates for the rural and urban areas and for both areas combined estimated from the survey data are similar to the level estimated by Rafiq (1979) for the 1971 census. It may be appropriate to point out here that the difference between the estimated crude birth rate of Agyei (1979) and that of Rafiq is due to the methods used. Rafiq used an indirect method based on the proportion of the female population in the total population, multiplying the product of the proportion and quantity (1 + sex ratio at birth) by the female birth rate. Agyei used the direct method (using the number of children born during the twelve months preceding the census date), which is similar to computing the crude birth rate from registered births. It is our opinion that the estimated level of the crude birth rate from the data of the 1980 census is rather too low when

Table 5.1: Estimated crude birth rates from censuses and survey data: Papua New Guinea

Source	Census year	Unadjusted rates/1000	Adjusted rates/1000
Van de Kaa	1966	44.0	45.9
Agyei	1971	44.7	47.5
Rafiq	1971	46.0	48.8
Bakker	1980	34.2[a]	—
Demographic survey	1979–1980		
Rural		47.0	47.0
Urban		46.0	46.0
All sectors		46.0	46.0

Note: a. The age–sex distribution data are not available for computing the adjusted crude birth rate.

Source: Based on data from surveys and censuses published by D.J. Van de Kaa, 1971;. W.K.A. Agyei, 1979; M. Rafiq, 1979; M.L. Bakker (no date).

considering the demographic parameters that are available for Papua New Guinea.

The crude birth rate as a measure of fertility is affected by differences in the age–sex structure of different populations. In order to control for the effects of age–sex differences on the crude birth rate, the United Nations (1956) offered a set of weights derived from the age pattern of fertility distribution. The age–sex adjusted crude birth rates (ASACBR) obtained for Papua New Guinea by applying these weights are given in Table 5.1. The adjusted rates are slightly higher for the censuses of 1966 and 1971 (data are not available for 1980) while the rates for the survey data remained the same. Also, while the estimation of the age–sex adjusted rate is based on weighted mean of women, that of the crude birth rate is based on the enumerated population. This obviously would create differences in the rates that are estimated using the two techniques. Besides, weights supplied by the UN model may themselves not be adequate for use with data from Papua New Guinea as it has been emphasised that the age–sex adjusted birth rate is a simple device for eliminating the effects of changes in the age–sex structure in the estimation of fertility, but could be affected by other factors (UN, 1956).

The estimated rates from the survey data appear to be very reasonable in comparison to those shown in Table 5.1. If we accept the adjusted rates as fairly accurate then fertility has changed only slightly from the 1971 level. In spite of the problems outlined above, it would be appropriate to assume that the level of fertility as measured by the crude birth rate is quite high (46 per 1000 mid-year population) for Papua New Guinea.

5.2.2 Levels and patterns of age-specific fertility and total fertility rates

The number of live births occurring to the female respondents aged between 15 and 49 in the twelve months prior to the survey were tabulated and used as the basis for estimating the levels and patterns of age-specific and total fertility rates. An age-specific fertility rate is the ratio of the births occurring to women of a particular age in a specified time period, usually a year, and the total number of years spent by women in that age group during the same period. These rates can be calculated by single years of age or by five-year age groups. The age-specific fertility rates derived from the survey data are shown in Table 5.2 with those estimated from the 1980 population census as the latter contained a similar question about fertility. There are marked differences between the two sets of data and caution must be exercised in comparing them because of the possible impact of variations in the methods of collecting and handling the data on the two occasions.

It must be stressed that the reliability of the estimates of both the survey and the census depends on the training of the interviewers and on the accurate reporting of the year of birth of recently born children as well as the age of the respondent. Also, the majority of enumerators used for the census to collect the information about fertility from the female respondents or heads of households were male while, in this survey, female interviewers interviewed female respondents.

Bearing these problems in mind, the pattern of fertility in Papua New Guinea as depicted by the survey and census data is similar (see Table 5.2). The main difference is found among the group aged between 15 and 19. The pattern can be described as an 'early marriage, high fertility' pattern. Fertility peaks occur between the ages of 20 and 29 and what is evident from the pattern is that fertility is relatively high at the extreme ages of childbearing; i.e. between 15 and 19 and between 45 and 49. The data also reveal that childbearing starts early and continues throughout the childbearing period.

The age-specific fertility pattern shown in Figure 2 conforms to the pattern commonly found in countries with high levels of fertility. According to the United Nations classification of peak age patterns of fertility (1963: 106), it conforms to the broad-peak type in which the maximum fertility occurs in the group aged between 20 and 29.

In countries with low levels of fertility, childbearing tends to be concentrated in a narrower range of ages than those with high levels of fertility. The proportion of births in the age range 20–34 to the total fertility in countries with such low fertility rates is usually 75 per cent or above (United Nations, 1963: 106). The observed pattern of fertility in this age range for Papua New Guinea is quite different from that in countries with low fertility levels described above as the data in this survey show that only 65 per cent of all births were in this age range in both rural and urban samples. In addition, the levels of fertility in the age range 35 and over are 26.5 and 28 per cent for the rural and urban respondents respectively.

Table 5.2: Age-specific fertility rates during the twelve months prior to the survey and census: Papua New Guinea

Age group	1979–80 Demographic survey			1980 Population census[a]		
	Rural	Urban	All sectors	Rural	Urban	All sectors
15–19	0.105	0.078	0.087	0.029	0.091	0.041
20–24	0.286	0.242	0.258	0.185	0.252	0.202
25–29	0.298	0.272	0.283	0.230	0.225	0.230
30–34	0.229	0.238	0.233	0.200	0.163	0.197
35–39	0.173	0.162	0.168	0.144	0.116	0.142
40–44	0.098	0.094	0.097	0.091	0.054	0.089
45–49	0.061	0.066	0.063	0.054	0.030	0.053
Total fertility rate	6.25	5.76	5.95	4.66	4.66	4.77
Gross reproduction rate	2.99	2.76	2.85	2.58	2.47	2.62
Net reproduction rate	2.25	2.08	2.18	1.94	2.10	2.01

Note: a. Taken from M.L. Bakker, Working Paper No. 7 — Preliminary fertility estimates derived from 1980 census data for geographical subdivisions of Papua New Guinea (No date).

Figure 2: Age-specific fertility rates for rural, urban and both sectors: Papua New Guinea

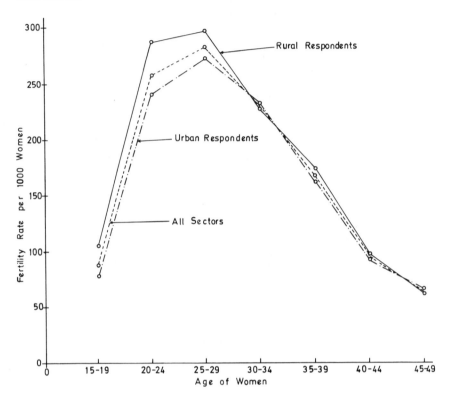

Source: Table 5.2 (demographic survey data 1979–80).

The total fertility rate is generally regarded as the best single cross-sectional measure of fertility because it is independent of the age composition of childbearing populations. Also, because it assumes that all women survive from birth to the end of the childbearing period, it is independent of the mortality level (Bogue, 1969). The total fertility rate is the sum of the age-specific fertility rates over the full childbearing ages (15–49). The total fertility rate represents the number of live births that would be possible if a woman were to experience the age-specific fertility rates of a given period throughout her reproductive years. The estimated total fertility rates from the survey and the data from the 1980 population census are presented in Table 5.2. The survey data show that a completed family size by age 49 is six children and the census shows that it is approximately five children. It must be noted that the total fertility rate is a hypothetical measure of fertility but, nevertheless, is a useful means of expressing the implication of recent period rates in terms of completed family size.

In addition to the direct estimation of the total fertility rates from the age-specific fertility rates, the total fertility rates have also been estimated using certain indirect techniques, such as those used by Coale and Demeny (1967), Brass (1968, 1975), the use of the average of P_1/F_1, P_2/F_2 and P_3/F_3; P_2/F_2, P_3/F_3 and P_4/F_4; or any other P_i/F_i ratio as the adjustment factors as well as the Brass technique (1979).

The Brass technique (1968, 1975) makes an adjustment for the problems of 'recall lapse' which are particularly important in the developing countries and arise because: (1) in societies where literacy levels are low, women often do not report their children who have grown up or those who have left home; (2) illiterate women are often unable to remember or even understand numbers accurately, with consequent misreporting of the total number of children they have borne — this problem tends to increase with the age of the women; (3) older women tend not to count offspring who died many years earlier and in some societies the women will not report any children who have died soon after birth.

Brass has shown that the reported average number of children ever born is frequently a downward-biased estimate of the cumulative fertility experience of women over 30 or 35 years old, and the average parity of women past 45 or 50 years old, being typically understated, would usually provide an under-estimate of total fertility (Brass *et al.*, 1968). On the other hand, younger women under 30 are assumed to report the total number of children ever born to them with much greater accuracy. This is because these women are not asked to recall events from the remote past or to count a large number of children. In addition, a higher proportion of the children ever born to younger women will have survived to the time of the survey and relatively few will have left the household.

Adoption is common throughout the societies of Papua New Guinea and may possibly affect the estimates of fertility. However, until there is a nationwide survey, it is difficult to know whether it significantly influences the distribution of children to mothers. Adoption is inextricably tied up with traditional exchange systems and, for the present, it will be assumed that it is primarily reciprocal with little impact on the overall fertility pattern.

The Brass method is used to estimate adjusted age-specific fertility rates and adjusted total fertility rates from the total number of children ever born and the number of children born during a fixed time period before the census or survey, usually during the preceding twelve months. The basic idea of the Brass method is that the data on the total number of children born by age of woman (P_i) give us an idea about the level of fertility which is sensitive to the problem of misreporting previously mentioned. On the other hand, the data for children

Table 5.3: A summary of estimates of total fertility rates by different techniques: Papua New Guinea

Technique employed	Rural	Urban	All sectors
Direct method	6.25	5.76	5.95
Coale and Demeny			
TFR $= P_3^2/P_2$	6.35	5.79	6.25
Brass			
TFR $= P_2 (P_2/P_3)^4$	5.94	5.08	5.53
Brass adjustment			
P_2/F_2 ratio	6.43	7.22	6.92
P_3/P_3 ratio	6.44	6.63	6.70
Other adjustments			
$\frac{1}{3}(P_1/F_1 + P_2/F_2 + P_3/F_3)$	6.23	6.35	6.52
$\frac{1}{3}(P_2/F_2 + P_3/F_3 + P_4/F_4)$	6.41	6.16	6.52

born more than twelve months prior to the census or survey (F_i) are sensitive to reference-period error. However, this latter error is likely to be common to all ages of women in any specific culture for a particular census or survey and the age-specific reports of children born during the preceding twelve-month period give an idea of the pattern of current fertility. Adjusting the latter against the former gives us a more accurate estimation of total fertility rate.

If we accept the previous assumption — that we can expect greater accuracy in reporting children born to younger women — the ratio between the mean number of children ever born to women under 30, particularly women in the age ranges 20–24 or 25–29 and their cumulated age-specific fertility may be used as a correction factor (i.e. P_2/F_2 or P_3/F_3). The correction factor is then applied to the age-specific fertility rates to yield a set of rates that reflects more accurately the true fertility level and pattern.

The technique is based on three basic assumptions: (1) that fertility patterns have been constant over time; (2) that the level of fertility is accurately reflected in the number of children ever born as reported by females under 30 years of age; (3) that the age pattern of fertility is accurately depicted by the data on the number of children born twelve months prior to the census or survey. The Brass method has been applied to the data in this survey and the estimates of the total fertility rates with those of the other techniques are presented in Table 5.3. The P_i/F_i ratios and the adjusted age-specific fertility rates are shown in Appendix C.

The total fertility rates estimated from the various methods appear not to be drastically different from those computed from the direct method. In addition, the estimates tend to be very close to the mean number of children ever born to the women in the 45–49 age group, which is taken as completed family size (see Table 5.4). These results provide strong assurance that the data are fairly good and that the fertility rates based on the data concerning the histories of pregnancy are fairly accurate, and do not overestimate the level of fertility in the recent past.

5.2.3 Selection of total fertility rates for the study areas

Several techniques have been used to estimate the total fertility rates in an attempt to obtain plausible levels of fertility for the study areas. From the several estimates of the total fertility rates in Table 5.3, the levels that should be considered appropriate for the study areas are still difficult to answer satisfactorily. This is so because all the techniques used operate under different assumptions which may not be satisfied explicitly by the data. An examination of the various estimates derived from the different methods suggests a total fertility rate of above six and probably closer to seven for both the rural and urban areas. The estimates produced by the Brass P_2/F_2 and P_3/F_3 ratios are regarded to be the most plausible estimates of total fertility rates for the study areas and possibly for Papua New Guinea.

5.2.4 Reproduction rates

The estimates for the gross reproduction rates and net reproduction rates are also given in Table 5.2. The gross reproduction rate is interpreted as showing the extent to which the generation of daughters would replace the preceding generation of mothers if fertility remained constant and if there were no deaths among females of reproductive age. The net reproduction rate is interpreted as showing the extent to which a generation of daughters would replace the preceding generation of females if fertility and mortality remained at constant levels. The gross and net reproduction rates for the rural and urban areas estimated from the survey data are approximately three and two respectively. This means that a Papua New Guinean woman living throughout the childbearing period replaces herself with about two daughters. Such a rate means an extremely rapid growth of the population.

5.3 CUMULATIVE FERTILITY

This section examines cumulative fertility which measures the number of children ever born up to the time of the survey. Cumulative fertility is normally referred to as the woman's current parity. For younger women, current parity will reflect their fertility during a limited period only, while for older women this measure comes close to completed fertility.

5.3.1 The mean number of children ever born

Estimates of the mean number of children ever born from the survey data are presented in Table 5.4 along with those estimated from the censuses of 1966 and

Table 5.4: Mean number of children ever born to women in specific age groups in the censuses of 1966 and 1971 and the demographic survey 1979–80: Papua New Guinea

Age group	Interval (i)	Population censuses 1966	1971	1979–1980 Demographic survey Rural	Urban	All sectors
15–19	1	0.259	0.186	0.154	0.141	0.145
20–24	2	1.320	1.343	1.351	1.329	1.338
25–29	3	2.680	2.783	2.929	2.775	2.891
30–34	4	3.660	3.386	4.241	3.881	4.123
35–39	5	4.280	4.432	5.102	4.586	4.933
40–44	6	4.520	4.662	5.609	5.348	5.554
45–49	7	4.430	4.606	6.484	6.067	6.338

1971 (those for the 1980 census were not available at the time of writing this report). Comparisons of the survey data with the estimates obtained from the 1966 and 1971 censuses seem to indicate that fertility has risen considerably since 1966 for all age groups except the 15–19 group, which showed a decline. It is plausible that the higher parity especially for the 30–34 age group through to the 45–49 age groups may be due partly to a rise in fertility from a reduction of the incidence of childlessness and partly to relatively more accurate data.

The number of children ever born increases steadily with the age of women for the survey data from the 15–19 age group to the 45–49 year age group. On the other hand, those for the two censuses show an increase up to the age of 44 but thereafter show a slight tendency to decline. The survey data also reveals a higher mean number of children ever born in the 25–29 age group to the 45–49 age group than the estimates for the censuses. The higher estimates of the mean number of children ever born from the survey data probably reflect more complete reporting of past births rather than any dramatic rise in fertility between the time of the censuses and this survey. The survey data were based on answers to a long and detailed set of questions about each female respondent's history of fertility, whereas the questions in the censuses simply enquired about the total number of children ever born, without attempting to investigate the entire history of fertility of the respondents in detail.

Four distinct patterns can be identified in the survey data (see Table 5.4. All sectors) with respect to the mean number of children ever born in the following groups. First, the respondents under 30, who are still in the midst of their childbearing life; second, the respondents 30–34, the cohort approaching completion of their childbearing period; third, the respondents between 35–44, the cohort in the last stages of fertility; fourth, the respondents aged 45 and over, the cohort with completed families. Each of these presents a unique fertility experience. The respondents under 30 have the least number of children, which is expected — under 3 children; those aged 30–34 show a high pattern in relation to their age group — approximately 4 children; the 35–44 year age group has between 5 and 5.5 children and, as expected, the older women aged 45 and over had 6 children or more.

5.4 DIFFERENTIALS IN FERTILITY

The study of differences in fertility between social, economic and other components of a population is the primary concern of most fertility surveys. In addition to the purely descriptive value, the identification of the direction and magnitude of fertility differentials is an essential first step towards an understanding of the determinants of fertility. There is evidence in the censuses of 1966, 1971 and 1980 and also in this survey of differential fertility among Papua New Guinean women of different demographic and socio-economic characteristics. These include differences according to place of residence, region of residence and educational attainment.

5.4.1 Rural–urban differentials

Analyses of the fertility data from the censuses of Papua New Guinea provide some evidence of rural–urban differentials. For example, Van de Kaa (1971) noted a higher rate of fertility in urban areas than in rural areas in his analysis of the data of the 1966 census. Rafiq (1979) also came to a similar conclusion when he analysed the data from the 1971 census. But Rafiq observed that the age composition of the population of urban areas was more conducive to higher fertility (as measured by the general fertility rate) than that of rural areas. It can be demonstrated without much difficulty that the general fertility rate would have been lower in urban areas than the level indicated by the data collected in the 1971 census had the age composition of rural areas been the same as that of the urban areas. The rural–urban fertility estimates provided by the data collected for the 1980 census in Table 5.2 (Bakker, n.d.) appear rather inconclusive.

The age-specific fertility rates derived from the survey data for the rural and urban areas are presented in Table 5.5. Fertility rates are higher for the rural respondents in all age groups except in the groups aged 30–34 and 45–49, where the rates are slightly higher for the urban respondents. The differences in the fertility rates are quite substantial, especially among the respondents aged under 25, in contrast to the older women aged 25–49 years old. These differences are not due to early marriages on the part of the rural respondents. As shown in Chapter 3, the mean age at first marriage for the rural and urban respondents are basically the same, 17.2 and 17.4 years respectively. The differences probably reflect the relatively more extensive use of contraceptives among the younger and educated urban respondents.

The age-specific fertility rates have been summed up and multiplied by a factor of five in Table 5.5 to give the total fertility rates (TFR), which represent the mean number of children that would be born to the respondents by the end of the childbearing period on the assumption that the current schedule of age-specific fertility continues unchanged. As can be seen in Table 5.5, the total fertility rate in rural areas is 8.5 per cent higher than the rate in urban areas; and the differences in the gross reproduction rate and the net reproduction rate are 8.3 per cent and 8.2 per cent respectively (see Table 5.2).

5.4.2 Children ever born

The data for the mean number of children ever born presented in Table 5.5 also suggests differences in fertility levels between the rural and urban areas, although the differences are not very pronounced among the respondents aged

Table 5.5: Distribution of mean number of children ever born and age-specific fertility rates in the twelve months prior to the survey and selected indicators of fertility: Papua New Guinea (Rural and urban areas)

Age group	Interval (i)	Mean number of children ever born per respondent		Age-specific fertility rate per respondent	
		Rural	Urban	Rural	Urban
15–19	1	0.154	0.141	0.105	0.078
20–24	2	1.351	1.329	0.286	0.242
25–29	3	2.929	2.775	0.298	0.272
30–34	4	4.241	3.881	0.229	0.238
35–39	5	5.102	4.586	0.173	0.162
40–44	6	5.609	5.348	0.098	0.094
45–49	7	6.484	6.067	0.061	0.066
Total				1.250	1.152
Selected indicators					
Total fertility rate (unadjusted)				6.250	5.760
Children ever born to women aged 45 and over				6.484	6.067
P_1/P_2				0.114	0.106
f_1/f_2				0.367	0.322

Source: Based on tables 5.2 and 5.4.

under 30 as for those aged 30 and over (30–49). This pattern probably reflects life-cycle effects (for example, that the rural–urban differences only emerge clearly in later years of childbearing) or there is a historical convergence of rural and urban fertility.

Table 5.5 reveals that the mean number of children ever born to women aged 45 and over (if we take that as reflecting completed family size) in both rural and urban areas are slightly higher than the total fertility rates for both areas. Unless births during the twelve months prior to the survey were less completely reported than births occurring in the more distant past, which seems unlikely, or unless the dates of the more recent births were inaccurately reported, the differences suggest a possible decline in age-specific fertility rates in recent years.

The rural–urban differences are less pronounced with respect to the mean number of children ever born (i.e. 3.7 per cent for completed family size) than is indicated by the total fertility rates. It is difficult to say which of these figures is an approximation of the true situation, and in interpreting the figures presented in Table 5.5, one has to bear in mind that both sets of figures may have been distorted by under-reporting of births.

5.4.3 Regional fertility differentials

Table 5.6 presents age-specific fertility and the total fertility rates for the survey data along with those estimated from the 1980 census. Although the variations within each set of data are not very pronounced, the variations between the two sets of data are very pronounced. Again, as discussed earlier, the age-specific fertility and total fertility rates estimated from the census data are rather lower than those estimated from the survey data. The variations among the youngest age group (15–19) for example, are very pronounced, the differences varying from 37 per cent for the Papua region to 437 per cent for the Highlands region below the estimates for the survey data in the same age group. In spite of the differences, the patterns are similar for both sets of data.

The rest of this section will be limited to a discussion of the survey data. Table 5.6 reveals that in the age groups 20–24 through to 35–39, the age-specific fertility rates for the Highlands and the New Guinea Mainland regions tend to be lower than the national rates as well as for those for the Papua and the New Guinea Islands regions. On the other hand, both the Papua and the New Guinea Islands regions recorded rates above the national level, with the Papua region displaying the greatest variation. The patterns of difference varied across the age groups. All in all, the greatest differentials are observed in the youngest (15–19) and (20–24) age groups.

In general, the variations in the total fertility rates among the four regions are consistent with the differences in the age-specific fertility rates. The total fertility rates ranged from a low of 5.44 children for the Highlands region to

Table 5.6: Age-specific fertility rates in the twelve months prior to the survey and the census by region: Papua New Guinea

Source and region	15–19	20–24	25–29	30–34	35–39	40–44	45–49	TFR
				Age of mother				
			Demographic survey data 1979–1980					
Papua New Guinea	0.087	0.258	0.283	0.233	0.168	0.097	0.063	5.95
Papua Region	0.097	0.270	0.296	0.270	0.179	0.098	0.056	6.33
Highlands	0.102	0.215	0.258	0.200	0.152	0.096	0.063	5.44
New Guinea Mainland	0.106	0.221	0.251	0.216	0.160	0.094	0.069	5.59
New Guinea Islands	0.089	0.261	0.285	0.238	0.173	0.093	0.060	6.00
			1980 Population census[a]					
Papua New Guinea	0.041	0.202	0.230	0.197	0.142	0.089	0.053	4.77
Papua Region	0.071	0.246	0.250	0.206	0.164	0.091	0.052	5.40
Highlands	0.019	0.160	0.211	0.188	0.142	0.091	0.061	4.36
New Guinea Mainland	0.033	0.193	0.231	0.192	0.121	0.083	0.038	4.45
New Guinea Islands	0.060	0.248	0.257	0.230	0.160	0.098	0.059	5.56

Source: Taken from M.L. Bakker, Working Paper No. 7 — Preliminary fertility estimates derived from 1980 census data for geographical subdivisions of Papua New Guinea (No date).

a high of 6.33 children for the Papua region. Only the Papua region recorded a higher total fertility rate than the national level. It must be noted that the Highlands region is a prime area of out-migration while the Papua and New Guinea Islands regions are heavy in-migration areas (Skeldon, 1979). It is probable that the lower fertility level exhibited in the Highlands region is due to the effect of out-migration.

5.4.4 Fertility differentials by educational attainment

This section focuses on the fertility differential and the level of education of the rural and urban respondents. It is generally expected not only that at any given point in time, fertility and educational levels are inversely related but also that improving educational levels of a given population in the course of socio-economic development will contribute to declining fertility. Education is, perhaps, the single most important variable in the study of differential fertility. Unlike other socio-economic variables such as income and occupation, formal education, once obtained, does not change over time. Furthermore, it is a direct and powerful index of a woman's status (Cho et al., 1970).

The relationship between the level of education and the mean number of children ever born estimated from the survey data is shown in Table 5.7. The data support the inverse relationship between fertility and education. The pattern of differences is one of decreasing fertility with increasing education. In the rural sample, the respondents who have had a primary education have a slightly lower fertility rate than those with no education. However, the respondents who have had a secondary and tertiary education show marked differences to those with a primary education only, especially in the age group 20–39. The differences among the youngest age group (15–19) and the older age groups (40–44 and 45–49) are not very large. The pattern for the urban sample is similar to the rural pattern, except that the differences for the older respondents aged 40–44 and 45–49 are relatively larger than those for the rural respondents in the same age groups.

The relatively larger differences between the mean number of children ever born to the respondents educated to secondary and tertiary levels and to those respondents with no education in both rural and urban areas suggests that if educational levels rise beyond the primary stage, stronger fertility differentials with respect to education will become clearly evident. In general, education promotes and facilitates the acceptance of new and progressive ideas and practices.

5.5 SUMMARY AND CONCLUSION

In this chapter, the fertility levels and patterns have been examined as well as

Table 5.7: Mean number of children ever born by level of education and place of residence: Papua New Guinea

Age group (1)	No education (2)		Primary education (3)		Secondary and tertiary (4)		Percentage difference		
							(a) (2) and (3)	(b) (2) and (4)	(c) (3) and (4)
Rural respondents									
15–19	(40)[a]	0.168	(86)	0.159	(34)	0.163	−5.3	−2.9	+2.5
20–24	(100)	1.457	(142)	1.330	(80)	1.231	−8.7	−15.5	−10.0
25–29	(115)	3.320	(153)	3.068	(81)	2.878	−7.6	−13.3	−6.2
30–34	(115)	4.684	(131)	4.405	(78)	4.076	−6.0	−13.0	−7.5
35–39	(106)	5.640	(123)	5.417	(65)	4.953	−4.0	−12.2	−8.6
40–44	(98)	6.007	(68)	5.860	(26)	5.711	−2.5	−4.9	−2.5
45–49	(79)	6.750	(45)	6.548	(20)	6.389	−3.0	−5.3	−2.4
Urban respondents									
15–19	(46)	0.156	(189)	0.152	(68)	0.151	−2.5	−3.2	−0.6
20–24	(118)	1.382	(261)	1.272	(175)	1.163	−7.9	−15.8	−8.6
25–29	(105)	3.206	(226)	2.980	(127)	2.751	−7.1	−14.2	−7.7
30–34	(83)	4.457	(119)	4.180	(71)	3.895	−6.2	−12.6	−6.8
35–39	(49)	5.526	(81)	5.250	(35)	4.912	−5.0	−11.1	−6.4
40–44	(31)	5.976	(28)	5.749	(20)	5.434	−3.8	−9.2	−5.7
45–49	(27)	6.662	(18)	6.496	(10)	6.012	−2.5	−9.8	−7.5

Note: a. The figures in parentheses represent the number of respondents on which the mean number of children ever born is based.

rural–urban, regional and educational differentials in Papua New Guinea. The results of the estimated fertility measures for the rural and urban areas of Papua New Guinea are high by world standards. Estimates of total fertility rates of 6.25 and 5.76, gross reproduction rates of 2.99 and 2.76 and net reproduction rates of 2.25 and 2.08 for the rural and urban areas respectively are high by the standards of the South Pacific islands. For example, Fiji's estimated total fertility rate was 3.50 in 1975, that of New Caledonia 5.30 in 1967 and that of Guam 4.80 in 1970.

The high level of fertility observed in Papua New Guinea may be interpreted in terms of social and cultural factors which favour high fertility. Marriage is the norm and women marry quite early. According to Bulmer (1971), no Papua New Guinean society favours the bearing of children by unmarried women. Marriage in Papua New Guinea is a complex term and must be interpreted to include civil, Christian and traditional marriages, consensual unions and polygamy as well as monogamy. Early marriage or early sexual union *per se* may not be a determinant of high fertility. However, in an agrarian society where the use of contraceptives is limited, the exposure to the risk of conception becomes greater and leads eventually to high levels of fertility.

It is important to point out, however, that there is some evidence of a possible decline in fertility levels as indicated by the more refined measures of fertility (for example, total fertility rate, gross and net reproduction rates). Even the adjusted total fertility rates are lower than those estimated from the 1971 population census.

The rural–urban comparison indicates that fertility is slightly lower among urban respondents than among the rural respondents. Although the fertility level in urban areas is lower than in rural areas, the former is still high by world standards. Nevertheless, it appears that urbanisation is beginning to have some impact on fertility levels in the urban areas (though very little).

Fertility differentials in the four regions of Papua New Guinea are less marked than those revealed by the rural–urban and educational differentials. The relatively lower fertility rates for the Highlands and New Guinea Mainland regions and the relatively higher fertility rates in the Papua and New Guinea Islands regions may be explained partly by differentials in out-migration and in-migration respectively.

Educational differentials are relatively quite significant in comparison to the rural–urban and regional differentials. The differentials are striking especially among the respondents in the 20–39 age group in both the rural and urban areas. Education is also showing a significant impact on fertility, but since education alone will take a long time to bring about changes in overall fertility levels, a well-organised family-planning programme is needed to arrest some of the socio-economic problems which promote high fertility.

It is anticipated that in Papua New Guinea within the next few decades the cohort of women of reproductive age (15–49) years old, which now has a low literacy rate, will be replaced by others with a relatively higher literacy rate. The age of marriage or sexual union, which is low, is likely to increase for both males and females. These undoubtedly will constitute very favourable factors for the future decline of fertility.

The phenomenon of modernisation is among the most important variables influencing fertility patterns in the world. Modernisation is taking place in Papua New Guinea, and the percentage of the urban population, as well as industrial employment, will increase tremendously in the next few decades. This trend of urbanisation and industrialisation can be expected to reduce the high level of fertility in Papua New Guinea in the coming decades.

6

Mortality Levels, Patterns and Differentials

6.1 INTRODUCTION

Mortality as a component of population change plays an important role in determining population growth. Significant declines in mortality have been observed in all parts of the world, but have occurred at different rates in different areas. In most of the developed countries, the mortality rate has completed the transition from a high to a low level, starting with a gradual decline in the early nineteenth century, an acceleration of this downward course in the late nineteenth century, tapering off to a relatively low level in the middle of the twentieth century. This took place over a period of about 150 years in the developed countries but is occurring in the Third-World countries at a much more rapid rate. In the Third-World countries the most significant fall in the death rate has taken place since World War II and is due to a combination of factors which were designed to bring about a more rapid decline in countries with high levels of mortality. These factors include the role of international health agencies, the use of antibiotics, the development of efficient methods for combating malaria and other communicable diseases and other benefits to health in the Third-World countries that have resulted from their contacts with the developed countries.

In Sri Lanka, for example, the crude death rate declined from 20.6 deaths per 1000 mid-year population in 1940 to 10.1 deaths per 1000 mid-year population in 1957 (Frederiksen, 1968) and was 6 per 1000 in 1982 (World Bank, 1984). The life expectancy increased from 43 years in 1940 to 69 years in 1982 (World Bank, 1984). Data such as these are important because they point to changes in a particular population. These facts indicate trends, differences or uniformities which assist in the long-term aim of extending the length of human life. Furthermore, these facts enable the areas of greatest concern to be more easily pinpointed for further research and better government action in providing additional health facilities.

Data for mortality in Papua New Guinea are scanty and unreliable. Estimates of mortality levels, patterns and differentials have been based on census reports and sample surveys of small areas, which provide a limited picture of the situation. Recent socio-economic development plans have emphasised the need for adequate and detailed data, first, to provide a better picture of mortality levels, patterns and differentials and second, to pinpoint areas where there is need for government action — for example, in the areas of infant and child mortality.

In view of these needs, this study was designed to obtain estimates of mortality (infant and child) from various sources, both direct and indirect, and arrive at a set of figures for mortality rates that would be consistent and would also contribute to a clearer understanding of mortality levels, patterns and differentials in Papua New Guinea.

The estimates of mortality levels, patterns and differentials in this chapter are based on: (1) the recorded retrospective fertility (number of children ever born) of all the female respondents; (2) any deaths recorded in each household in the twelve months preceding the survey; (3) a complete pregnancy history of each female respondent; (4) the recorded age–sex structure of the survey population.

6.2 CRUDE DEATH RATES

The estimates of the crude death rates and infant mortality rates by the direct method in this section are based on the number of deaths recorded in each household in the twelve months preceding the survey. A serious drawback of collecting data on mortality is that it is based on what the respondents can remember. Admittedly, there are some inherent problems in the collection of data and in cultural characteristics relating to the reporting of deaths in censuses and surveys. Accordingly, it should be noted that the estimates of mortality presented here do not give conclusive information and the lack of suitable data in Papua New Guinea has made comparisons impossible.

Table 6.1 shows the crude death rates in terms of sex, region, and whether rural or urban. The data reveal the following differences. Males tend to have higher mortality rates than the females in terms of regions and rural and urban areas. This finding confirms the change in mortality levels observed in the 1971 population census. In 1966, life expectancy at birth for males exceeded that for females; in 1971 the reverse was true. The estimated crude death rates are highest for the Highlands region and lowest for the New Guinea Islands region. The urban mortality level was 25 per cent lower than the rural mortality level. The rural–urban differential may be justified on the basis of the availability of better health services and the concentration of health-service personnel in the urban areas. The regional differences may be due to differences in socio-economic development.

Table 6.1: Population size, number of deaths and crude death rates with regard to sex, region and rural or urban residence: Papua New Guinea 1979–80

Region/area	Population			Number of deaths			Crude death rates		
	Males	Females	Both sexes	Males	Females	Both sexes	Males	Females	Both sexes
Papua	5,004	3,491	8,495	66	36	102	13.2	10.3	12.0
Highlands	6,527	6,110	12,637	110	82	192	16.8	13.4	15.2
New Guinea Mainland	5,874	6,982	12,856	96	88	184	16.3	12.6	14.3
New Guinea Islands	4,350	5,237	9,587	54	52	106	12.4	9.9	11.0
Rural	10,327	10,873	21,200	173	153	326	16.8	14.0	15.4
Urban	11,428	10,947	22,375	153	105	258	13.4	9.6	11.5
All regions/areas	21,755	21,820	43,575	326	258	584	15.0	11.8	13.4

Table 6.2: Number of births, infant deaths and infant-mortality rates with regard to sex, region and rural or urban residence: Papua New Guinea 1979–80

Region/area	Number of live births			Number of infant deaths			Infant mortality rates[a]		
	Males	Females	Both sexes	Males	Females	Both sexes	Males	Females	Both sexes
Papua	198	184	382	18	16	34	91.0	87.0	89.0
Highland	296	276	572	32	26	58	108.1	94.2	101.4
New Guinea Mainland	317	294	611	32	27	59	101.0	91.8	96.6
New Guinea Islands	236	220	456	20	16	36	84.7	72.7	78.9
Rural	536	460	996	57	44	101	106.3	95.6	101.4
Urban	511	514	1025	45	41	86	88.1	79.8	83.9
All regions/areas	1047	974	2021	102	85	187	97.4	89.8	92.5

Note: a. Infant mortality rates are given per 1000 live births.

6.2.1 Current infant mortality rates

Table 6.2 presents infant mortality rates based on the reported number of births and deaths in the twelve months preceding the survey. Again, as with the crude death rate, the infant mortality rate is highest for the Highlands region and lowest for the New Guinea Islands region. The level of infant mortality for female infants is lower than that for male infants. This pattern is similar to that for the crude death rate. The pattern suggests that mortality has probably declined more sharply for females than for the males between 1966 and 1980.

Table 6.3 presents infant mortality rates in relationship to age and place of residence of mother. As expected, the infant mortality rate in both the youngest age group (15–19) and the oldest (45–49) is higher than in the group aged 20–24 in the rural areas. The rates increase steadily after the 20–24 year age group to a rate of 130.4 per 1000 live births for the group aged 45–49. In other words, children born to the youngest and oldest mothers are more likely to die than children born to mothers aged 20 to 24. The rural infant-mortality rates show a consistent pattern which, apart from that of the 15–19 year age group, increases with age.

The infant mortality rates for the urban areas are slightly different from those of the rural areas. The lowest infant mortality rate was recorded for mothers in the 30–34 year age group. Although Ruzicka and Kanitkar (1973) found the lowest infant mortality rate among mothers aged between 30 and 34 in their Bombay study, the rate for the urban areas in Papua New Guinea is considered to be suspect. This is due to under-reporting of infant deaths or age, or misreporting, or both.

Table 6.4 also shows estimated infant mortality rates for the 1971 and 1980 censuses, together with the data from this survey to compare the four geographical regions of Papua New Guinea. The patterns for the three sets of data are similar and the levels have declined for all the regions between 1971 and 1980. This is expected, but the magnitude of the declines in infant mortality rates between 1971 and 1980 based on the estimates of the two censuses is rather dramatic. In other words, the estimated infant mortality rates based on the data from the 1980 census are rather too low. This could be due to under-reporting of infant deaths in the census or misreporting ages, or both.

6.3 ESTIMATION OF INFANT MORTALITY RATES FROM THE NUMBER OF CHILDREN EVER BORN AND THE NUMBER OF CHILDREN WHO SURVIVE[1]

Feeney's (1976) method for estimating infant mortality rates from the proportion

---

1. The basic data used for this analysis is presented in appendices D1 and D2.

Table 6.3: Infant mortality rates by current age and residence of mother: Papua New Guinea 1979–80

Age of mother	Number of live births			Number of deaths			Rate per 1000 live births		
	Rural	Urban	All sectors	Rural	Urban	All sectors	Rural	Urban	All sectors
15–19	84	77	161	9	7	16	107.1	90.9	99.4
20–24	220	208	428	20	17	37	90.9	81.7	86.4
25–29	257	260	517	25	20	45	97.3	76.9	87.0
30–34	180	201	381	18	15	33	100.0	74.6	86.6
35–39	137	134	271	14	12	26	102.1	89.5	95.9
40–44	68	84	152	8	8	16	117.6	95.2	105.3
45–49	46	58	104	6	7	13	130.4	120.7	125.0
Not stated	4	3	7	1		1	—	—	—
All ages	996	1025	2021	101	86	187	101.4	83.9	92.5

Table 6.4: Infant mortality rates[a] by sex and region: Papua New Guinea 1971, 1979–80 and 1980

Region	1971 Population census[b]			1980 Population census[b]			1979 to 1980 Demographic survey[b]		
	Males	Females	Both sexes	Males	Females	Both sexes	Males	Females	Both sexes
Papua	115.0	101.0	108.0	60.0	56.0	58.0	91.0	87.0	89.0
Highlands	160.0	141.0	151.0	95.0	74.0	85.0	108.1	94.2	101.4
New Guinea Mainland	147.0	134.0	141.0	80.0	72.0	76.0	101.0	91.8	96.6
New Guinea Islands	86.0	75.0	81.0	53.0	49.0	52.0	84.7	72.7	78.9
All regions	142.0	125.0	134.0	78.0	66.0	72.0	97.4	89.8	92.5

Notes: a. Infant mortality rates are given per 1000 live births.
b. Taken from M.L. Bakker, Working Paper No. 4 — Spatial Differentiation of Mortality in PNG. A. Classification Based on the Results of the 1980 Census (No date).
Source: Table 6.2.

of deceased children is applied in this section to estimate infant mortality rates for rural and urban areas and the four mian geographical regions of Papua New Guinea. The method, in addition to the values of the proportion of deceased children (D_i), uses the value of M (mean age at childbearing) which is obtained from the mean parity ratios for successive five-year age groups of women. The method also provides an estimate for the 'years prior to the census or survey' to which the estimating of the infant mortality rate applies. The infant mortality rates are computed for five-year age groups starting with the group aged 20 to 24 through to the age group aged 45 to 49.

The method is based on the equation:

$$D_i = 1 - \sum_j C_j (M)P_j(\omega,r)$$

where:

D_i = the proportion of deceased children born to women in a particular age group i

C_j = the proportion of these children who were born in the j-th year prior to the census or survey (Feeney estimates C_j, using M)

$P_j(\omega,r)$ = The proportion of children born during the j-th year prior to the census or survey who would survive to the time of the census or survey if:

(1) IMR $= \omega$ at the time of the census or survey and had been declining at a constant rate (r), in the years before the census or survey;
(2) there was no mortality differential by age of mother;
(3) the mortality experience during each year preceding the census or survey can be approximated by an available one-parameter model life table family.

6.3.1 Levels and patterns of infant mortality

The levels and patterns of the estimated infant mortality rates are presented in Tables 6.5 and 6.6 for the rural–urban and the four geographical regions of Papua New Guinea respectively. Since infant mortality estimated for the 15–19 year age group is particularly liable to errors due to the small number of children born, and as this age group has an above-average infant-mortality risk, the rate is not presented in the estimates. It is important to point out that the estimates given in Tables 6.5 and 6.6 may have been affected by omission errors which characterise retrospective data collected in the developing countries (Brass *et al.*, 1968).

It is evident from the estimates (see Tables 6.5 and 6.6) that, over the past

Table 6.5: Infant mortality rates and year to which the estimate applies from the number of children ever born by current age and residence of mother: Papua New Guinea 1979–80

Age of mother	Rural			Urban			All sectors		
	Proportion dead	Infant mortality	Year	Proportion dead	Infant mortality	Year	Proportion dead	Infant mortality	Year
15–19	0.110	–	–	0.056	–	–	0.083	–	–
20–24	0.117	94.6	1977.4	0.109	86.6	1977.3	0.113	90.0	1977.3
25–29	0.141	98.8	1976.6	0.137	95.1	1975.4	0.138	96.0	1975.4
30–34	0.159	101.4	1973.4	0.157	99.5	1973.2	0.158	101.1	1973.3
35–39	0.182	109.1	1970.8	0.167	98.8	1970.6	0.175	104.0	1970.6
40–44	0.207	115.2	1967.8	0.189	103.6	1967.5	0.198	109.0	1967.5
45–49	0.236	118.7	1964.5	0.227	112.8	1964.2	0.232	115.5	1964.3

Table 6.6: Infant mortality rates and year to which the estimate applies from the number of children ever born by current age of mother and region: Papua New Guinea 1979–80

Region: Age of mother	Papua			Highlands			New Guinea Mainland			New Guinea Islands		
	Prop. dead	Infant mort.	Year	Prop. dead	Infant mort.	Year	Prop. dead	Infant mort.	Year	Prop. dead	Infant mort.	Year
15–19	0.081	–	–	0.091	–	–	0.092	–	–	0.075	–	–
20–24	0.112	89.1	1977.3	0.118	95.1	1977.4	0.115	92.6	1977.4	0.107	85.0	1977.3
25–29	0.137	95.2	1975.4	0.142	99.4	1975.5	0.138	96.5	1975.5	0.137	95.1	1975.4
30–34	0.157	99.5	1973.2	0.164	105.5	1973.3	0.160	102.0	1973.3	0.150	95.0	1973.2
35–39	0.172	102.0	1970.6	0.182	109.0	1970.8	0.179	107.0	1970.8	0.165	97.6	1970.6
40–44	0.190	104.2	1967.5	0.209	116.2	1967.7	0.205	113.8	1967.7	0.180	98.3	1967.5
45–49	0.229	113.9	1964.2	0.247	124.3	1964.4	0.243	122.1	1964.4	0.208	102.8	1964.3

15 years, infant mortality has declined consistently in Papua New Guinea. The percentage decline between 1964 and 1977 for the rural areas was 20 per cent that for the urban areas was 22 per cent respectively. With regards to the geographical regions, the decline was highest for the New Guinea Mainland region — a 24 per cent decline in this period. The Highlands region is next with a 23 per cent decline, then Papua with a decline of 22 per cent and the New Guinea Islands region with 17 per cent. In other words, the Highlands and the New Guinea Mainland regions, which are relatively worse off in terms of infant mortality, experienced the greatest decline during the 15 years prior to this survey.

The patterns of infant mortality for the rural and urban areas are basically the same except for the 35–39 age group in urban areas, where the infant mortality rate is approximately the same as that in the 30–34 age group. This is unexpected and may be due to under-reporting of deceased children in the 35–39 age group. Two patterns are evident in the regional data. The Highlands and the New Guinea Mainland regions have a relatively high infant mortality rate compared with the Papua and New Guinea Islands regions. Accordingly, the Highlands and the New Guinea Mainland regions show a similar infant mortality pattern and the Papua and the New Guinea Islands regions have a similar pattern.

6.3.2 Differentials in infant mortality

Differentials by current age and place of residence of the mother have been discussed briefly in section 6.2.1. However, the indirect estimates give some additional differentials. Differentials by sex of child, rural–urban residence, as well as geographical regions are focused upon in this section.

It is generally accepted that there is a higher rate of mortality amongst males than females at every age, except where the rate of maternal mortality is rather high. The estimated infant mortality rates presented in Table 6.7 show that male infants are more vulnerable and likely to die than female infants in the first year of life. Although the sex differential holds for rural–urban residence as well as on a regional basis, the differences are not very pronounced. Nevertheless, the rates for the age groups between 45 and 49 are relatively higher than those for the younger women.

In most countries infant mortality is relatively low in urban areas and high in rural areas. A comparison of the data presented in Table 6.5 shows that in Papua New Guinea infants in urban areas have only a slight advantage of surviving over those born in rural areas. This advantage reflects differentials in many associated characteristics such as standard of living, access to health facilities, knowledge and economic ability for child care.

The regional differentials are presented in Table 6.6. The estimates of infant mortality rates indicate that the Papua and the New Guinea islands regions are

Table 6.7: Estimated infant mortality rates by sex, region and residence of mother: Papua New Guinea 1979–80

| Age of mother | Region | | | | | | | | Residence | | | | | |
| | Papua | | Highlands | | New Guinea Mainland | | New Guinea Islands | | Rural | | Urban | | All sectors | |
	Males	Females	Males	Females	Males	Females	Males	Females	Males	Females	Males	Females	Males	Females
20–24	92.3	86.6	98.7	91.3	97.1	88.8	88.3	81.7	96.4	90.4	89.9	83.3	96.4	83.8
25–29	96.6	93.0	101.0	97.4	99.0	94.5	97.3	93.0	99.4	96.7	97.3	93.0	98.0	94.5
30–34	102.7	96.2	108.0	100.8	107.3	98.1	98.2	91.6	104.0	97.5	102.7	95.6	104.0	96.2
35–39	103.3	100.7	111.0	107.8	108.5	105.3	98.8	96.3	109.7	107.2	100.7	97.6	109.0	99.5
40–44	105.4	103.0	118.2	114.6	115.8	112.2	100.1	96.5	116.7	112.8	105.4	101.9	110.8	107.2
45–49	118.7	109.1	129.4	119.7	126.7	117.6	106.5	98.5	121.9	113.9	117.1	108.6	119.7	110.7

in an advantageous position in that their infant mortality rates are lower than those for the Highlands and the New Guinea Mainland regions. The data reveal some substantial differences between the New Guinea Islands region and the other three regions. The New Guinea Islands region exhibits the lowest infant mortality rates for the four regions. As a matter of fact, the infant mortality rates for the New Guinea Islands region are similar to those estimated for the urban areas in Table 6.5, except among the groups aged 40 to 44 and 45 to 49, in which the rates are lower for the New Guinea Islands region. The differences between the New Guinea Islands region and the other three regions may be attributed to the higher standards of education and higher economic levels characterising several areas of the New Guinea Islands region and also better health services.

6.4 ESTIMATION OF CHILD MORTALITY RATES USING DATA CLASSIFIED BY AGE OF MOTHER[2]

6.4.1. The method of estimation

The method employed in this section of our analysis is the refined Brass method (1968) (Trussell's method 1975) discussed in detail in Chapter 3 of the United Nations Manual X (1983). Basically, the method involves the conversion of the proportion dead (D_i) among children of women of different age groups from 15–19 to 45–49 years old to probabilities of dying from birth to age x, $q(x)$, for each group. The Brass estimation equation is given as:

$$D_i = CD_i/CEB_i \tag{1}$$

where:

D_i = the proportion of deceased (dead) children born to women in a particular age group i

CD_i = the number of children dead reported by women in age group i

CEB_i = the number of children ever borne by women in age group i

i = 15–19, 20–24, . . ., 45–49 years old

$$k(i) = a(i) + b(i)P(1)/P(2) + c(i)P(2)/P(3) \tag{2}$$

where:

$k(i)$ = mortality multiplier

---

2. The basic data for this analysis is presented in appendices D_1 and D_2.

$a(i)$, $b(i)$ and $c(i)$ are regression coefficients (Trussell variant) for estimating the multipliers based on the four different families of model life tables in the Coale-Demeny (1966) system.

$P(1)$, $P(2)$ and $P(3)$ refer to parities to the age groups 15–19, 20–24 and 25–29.

$$q(x) = k(i)D_i \qquad (3)$$

For example, we obtain the probability of dying at age 1 from women in the 15–19 age group, the probability of dying at age 2 from women in the 20–24 age group and so on up to age 20 from women in the 45–49 year age group. In addition, we obtain the probability of surviving from birth to exact age x, i.e. $1(x) = 1.0 - q(x)$. The method also provides a reference period, $t(x)$, i.e. the number of years prior to the census or survey, of each $q(x)$ estimate. The mortality multipliers, $k(i)$, used for the adjustmet of the proportion dead, D_i, for the effects of the age pattern of childbearing are computed from equation (2) above. And the regression coefficients (Trussell variant) used are those of the 'West' family model life tables. The choice of the 'West' model life tables is based on known parameters of fertility and mortality schedules for the population of Papua New Guinea. It was used by several researchers who analysed the data from the censuses for Papua New Guinea (see for example Van de Kaa, 1971; Agyei, 1979; Rafiq, 1979; McDevitt, 1979) because it minimised the danger of under-estimating child mortality. The computed multipliers are presented in Tables 6.8A and 6.8B for the rural–urban areas and the regions respectively.

Our estimates of the probabilities of dying, $q(x)$ and surviving, $1(x)$ are presented in Tables 6.9A and 6.9B for rural–urban residence and regional location. As the estimates obtained from the 15–19 age group are not very reliable, the estimates obtained from the group aged 20–24 years old are usually taken to be closest to reality. It should be noted that assuming that there is declining mortality, the children born to the older women will have experienced a higher mortality rate than children born to the younger women. The decline in child mortality levels between the estimates corresponding to the younger and older women (see Tables 6.9A and 6.9B) indicates that the children born to older women were experiencing higher mortality levels (as indicated by higher probabilities of dying). It is unlikely that this pattern is due to reporting errors since it is reasonable to assume that the proportion dead would be less completely reported by older women as 'recall lapse' tends to increase with older women.

Table 6.8A: Trussell's multipliers for child-mortality estimation, West model (rural and urban): Papua New Guinea 1979–80

Age of mother	Interval	Multipliers k(i) for:								
		Rural areas			Urban areas			All sectors		
		Males	Females	Both sexes	Males	Females	Both sexes	Males	Females	Both sexes
15–19	1	1.1874	1.1853	1.1863	1.2241	1.2183	1.2213	1.2052	1.2003	1.2029
20–24	2	1.0727	1.0740	1.0734	1.0725	1.0733	1.0729	1.0757	1.0763	1.0760
25–29	3	1.0639	1.0005	0.9997	0.9908	0.9928	0.9918	0.9979	0.9995	0.9987
30–34	4	1.0008	1.0018	1.0017	0.9911	0.9933	0.9922	0.9988	1.0006	0.9997
35–39	5	1.0154	1.0172	1.0163	1.0049	1.0072	1.0060	1.0129	1.0149	1.0138
40–44	6	1.0022	1.0040	1.0032	0.9913	0.9937	0.9925	0.9996	1.0015	1.0005
45–49	7	0.9949	0.9965	0.9958	0.9842	0.9865	0.9853	0.9923	0.9942	0.9931
P(1)/P(2)		0.1142	0.1138	0.1140	0.1057	0.1065	0.1061	0.1080	0.1087	0.1083
P(2)/P(3)		0.4632	0.4592	0.4612	0.4812	0.4765	0.4789	0.4647	0.4608	0.4628

Table 6.8B: Trussell's multipliers for child mortality estimation, West model (regional): Papua New Guinea 1979–80

Age Group	Interval (i)	Multipliers k(i) for:											
		Papua Region			Highlands Region			New Guinea Mainland Region			New Guinea Islands Region		
		Males	Females	Both sexes	Males	Females	Both sexes	Males	Females	Both sexes	Males	Females	Both sexes
15–19	1	1.1971	1.1965	1.1967	1.2206	1.2182	1.2194	1.1737	1.1740	1.1739	1.2157	1.2149	1.2152
20–24	2	1.0719	1.0731	1.0724	1.0696	1.0709	1.0702	1.0846	1.0859	1.0853	1.0693	1.0705	1.0699
25–29	3	0.9959	0.9972	0.9966	0.9887	0.9904	0.9896	1.0132	1.0144	1.0138	0.9894	0.9909	0.9855
30–34	4	0.9975	0.9988	0.9982	0.9895	0.9913	0.9905	1.0146	1.0158	1.0153	0.9905	0.9919	0.9912
35–39	5	1.0119	1.0131	1.0126	1.0033	1.0051	1.0042	1.0295	1.0306	1.0301	1.0043	1.0056	1.0051
40–44	6	0.9987	0.9999	0.9994	0.9897	0.9917	0.9907	1.0169	1.0177	1.0171	0.9909	0.9923	0.9916
45–49	7	0.9914	0.9927	0.9920	0.9826	0.9845	0.9836	1.0088	1.0099	1.0094	0.9839	0.9852	0.9846
P(1)/P(2)		0.1125	0.1118	0.1122	0.1085	0.1082	0.1084	0.1093	0.1083	0.1088	0.1099	0.1092	0.1096
P(2)/P(3)		0.4700	0.4667	0.4684	0.4866	0.4823	0.4845	0.4282	0.4250	0.4266	0.4851	0.4815	0.4833

Table 6.9A: Estimates of probabilities of dying and of surviving by sex derived from child-survival data classified by age of mother, West model (rural and urban): Papua New Guinea 1979–80

| Age group | Age | Probabilities of dying, q(x), and of surviving, l(x) | | | | | |
| | | Males | | Females | | Both sexes | |
	(x)	q(x)	l(x)	q(x)	l(x)	q(x)	l(x)
Rural areas							
15–19	1	0.1354	0.8646	0.1268	0.8732	0.1305	0.8695
20–24	2	0.1298	0.8702	0.1203	0.8797	0.1256	0.8744
25–29	3	0.1521	0.8479	0.1381	0.8619	0.1409	0.8591
30–34	5	0.1641	0.8359	0.1533	0.8467	0.1593	0.8407
35–39	10	0.1868	0.8132	0.1821	0.8179	0.1850	0.8150
40–44	15	0.2114	0.7886	0.2038	0.7962	0.2077	0.7923
45–49	20	0.2427	0.7573	0.2262	0.7738	0.2350	0.7650
Urban areas							
15–19	1	0.0685	0.9315	0.0707	0.9293	0.0696	0.9304
20–24	2	0.1212	0.8788	0.1127	0.8873	0.1169	0.8831
25–29	3	0.1387	0.8613	0.1330	0.8670	0.1359	0.8641
30–34	5	0.1606	0.8394	0.1500	0.8500	0.1558	0.8442
35–39	10	0.1708	0.8292	0.1662	0.8338	0.1680	0.8320
40–44	15	0.1903	0.8097	0.1848	0.8152	0.1876	0.8124
45–49	20	0.2313	0.7687	0.2160	0.7840	0.2237	0.7763
All sectors							
15–19	1	0.1145	0.8855	0.0840	0.9160	0.0998	0.9002
20–24	2	0.1302	0.8698	0.1119	0.8881	0.1216	0.8784
25–29	3	0.1407	0.8593	0.1349	0.8651	0.1378	0.8622
30–34	5	0.1638	0.8362	0.1511	0.8489	0.1579	0.8421
35–39	10	0.1854	0.8146	0.1695	0.8305	0.1774	0.8226
40–44	15	0.2009	0.7991	0.1953	0.8047	0.1981	0.8019
45–49	20	0.2382	0.7618	0.2217	0.7783	0.2304	0.7698

6.4.2 Levels and patterns of child mortality

The current levels and patterns of child mortality are clearly depicted in Tables 6.9A and 6.9B. As noted previously, the estimates show that child mortality levels have declined from those reported by older women (e.g. $_{20}q_0$) to those reported by younger women (e.g. $_3q_0$ or $_2q_0$). Special mention must be made of mortality levels corresponding to $_1q_0$ estimates. Some of the estimates in this category (see Table 6.9A) do not fit into the overall pattern of declining levels with estimates based on women of increasing age. This is due to the fact that the $_1q_0$ estimates derived from the method used are probably inflated because they rely heavily on births to very young mothers which are disproportionately first order births.

Normally the value of $_2q_0$ is taken as the index of the level of child mortality, rather than the value $_1q_0$ because the relation between $_2q_0$ and mortality rates at later ages are more stable, and accordingly $_2q_0$ is a better

Table 6.9B: Estimates of probabilities of dying and of surviving, by sex derived from child-survival data classified by age of mother, West model (regional): Papua New Guinea 1979–80

Age group	Age (x)	Probabilities of dying, q(x), and of surviving, l(x)					
		Males		Females		Both sexes	
		q(x)	l(x)	q(x)	l(x)	q(x)	l(x)
		Papua Region					
15–19	1	0.1101	0.8899	0.0823	0.9177	0.0969	0.9031
20–24	2	0.1243	0.8757	0.1170	0.8830	0.1201	0.8799
25–29	3	0.1384	0.8616	0.1336	0.8664	0.1365	0.8635
30–34	5	0.1616	0.8384	0.1518	0.8482	0.1567	0.8433
35–39	10	0.1760	0.8240	0.1722	0.8278	0.1742	0.8258
40–44	15	0.1918	0.8082	0.1880	0.8120	0.1899	0.8101
45–49	20	0.2360	0.7640	0.2184	0.7816	0.2271	0.7729
		Highlands Region					
15–19	1	0.1086	0.8914	0.1133	0.8867	0.1110	0.8890
20–24	2	0.1305	0.8695	0.1210	0.8790	0.1263	0.8737
25–29	3	0.1423	0.8577	0.1377	0.8623	0.1405	0.8595
30–34	5	0.1672	0.8328	0.1566	0.8434	0.1624	0.8376
35–39	10	0.1856	0.8144	0.1809	0.8191	0.1828	0.8172
40–44	15	0.2098	0.7902	0.2043	0.7953	0.2071	0.7929
45–49	20	0.2515	0.7485	0.2343	0.7657	0.2429	0.7571
		New Guinea Mainland Region					
15–19	1	0.1127	0.8873	0.1021	0.8979	0.1080	0.8920
20–24	2	0.1302	0.8698	0.1194	0.8806	0.1248	0.8752
25–29	3	0.1429	0.8571	0.1369	0.8631	0.1399	0.8601
30–34	5	0.1705	0.8295	0.1564	0.8436	0.1624	0.8376
35–39	10	0.1863	0.8137	0.1814	0.8186	0.1844	0.8156
40–44	15	0.2115	0.7885	0.2055	0.7945	0.2085	0.7915
45–49	20	0.2532	0.7468	0.2363	0.7637	0.2453	0.7547
		New Guinea Islands Region					
15–19	1	0.0973	0.9027	0.0850	0.9150	0.0911	0.9089
20–24	2	0.1187	0.8813	0.1103	0.8897	0.1145	0.8855
25–29	3	0.1385	0.8615	0.1328	0.8672	0.1350	0.8650
30–34	5	0.1535	0.8465	0.1438	0.8562	0.1487	0.8513
35–39	10	0.1677	0.8323	0.1639	0.8361	0.1658	0.8342
40–44	15	0.1813	0.8187	0.1756	0.8244	0.1785	0.8215
45–49	20	0.2115	0.7885	0.1970	0.8030	0.2048	0.7952

guide to the selection of a model life table than the $_1q_0$ value. Assuming that there is a declining rate of mortality. the $_2q_0$ estimate, which is based on women aged between 20 and 24, reflects child mortality to a more recent time period and presumably a higher model life-table level (corresponding to a lower mortality level) than would be the case for the $_3q_0$ or $_5q_0$ estimates, which are based on children ever born to women five to ten years older.

The probabilities of dying between birth and birthday $x(_xq_0)$ estimated from the proportion dead and corresponding values of expectation of life at birth

Table 6.10: Probabilities of dying between birth and birthday x($_xq_0$), computed from proportion dead and expectation of life ($^0e_0$): Papua New Guinea

Age (x)	$_xq_0$ Based on			$^0e_0$ Based on 1966[a] census data		$^0e_0$ Based on 1971[a] census data		$^0e_0$ Based on 1979–1980 Survey Data	
	1966[a]	1971[a]	1979–1980[b]	Males	Females	Males	Females	Males	Females
2	0.199	0.163	0.122	43.7	43.5	48.1	48.3	52.5	55.8
3	0.215	0.179	0.138	43.7	43.9	47.8	48.3	52.3	54.0
5	0.236	0.199	0.158	43.5	44.0	47.3	48.0	51.1	53.5
10	0.272	0.223	0.177	41.9	42.6	46.5	47.0	50.2	53.0
15	0.291	0.246	0.198	41.5	42.4	45.5	46.5	49.8	51.5
20	0.331	0.271	0.230	39.8	40.9	44.9	46.2	47.8	50.8

Sources: a. Based on M. Rafiq, 'Recent Demographic Changes in Papua New Guinea; Population studies 33 (1979), p. 309.
b. Based on Table 6.9A, all sectors q(x) for both sexes.

($^0e_0$) based on the 'West'-model life tables are given in Table 6.10 to provide further information on the levels and trends in child mortality in Papua New Guinea. The increases in the $^0e_0$ values in the period between 1966 and 1979 to 1980 suggest rapid declines in mortality in general. The $^0e_0$ values also suggest that mortality had fallen faster for the females than for the males. On the whole, female $^0e_0$ values based on the data from the 1971 census and this survey reveal higher longevity than for males in each age group. Nevertheless, the female longevity advantage decreases as age advances.

The reference period, t(x) to which the estimates of child mortality refer are given in Tables 6.11A and 6.11B. The t(x) values imply that the estimates of q(2), q(3), etc, refer to the mortality experiences prevalent approximately one year, two years, four years and six and a half years before the survey respectively, thereafter the estimated t(x) values increase by two and three-quarters to approximately three years per age group. The t(x) values are consistent with the notion that because the q(1) estimate, for example, is based on information about fertility corresponding to women in the 15–19 age group whose fertility experience is very recent, the q(1) estimate should also refer to the recent experience of the population (United Nations, 1983). The pattern of the t(x) values for the rural and urban areas, all sectors, and the four geographical regions is basically the same with very little variation, especially in the case of the t(x) values for the New Guinea Mainland region.

The 'West'-mortality levels with their corresponding reference dates for the rural and urban areas and the four regions are shown in Tables 6.12A and 6.12B. If the estimates of q(1) are disregarded because they are associated with relatively low levels in the Coale-Demeny model life tables, it can be seen that the estimates of the levels decline steadily, except in a few cases, with an increasing age of mother suggesting that child mortality has been declining. The reference dates presented in Tables 6.12A and 6.12B show the child mortality trends for male and female children. The data reveal that between approximately 1964 and 1977 child mortality has been declining for both male and female children.

6.4.3 Differentials in child mortality

Several features of Tables 6.9A and 6.9B are worthy of note in terms of differentials. First, the results indicate sex differentials in child mortality. Child mortality rates for female children are generally lower than those for the male children in the rural and urban areas as well as in all the regions. This conforms to the findings in most other populations, a slightly higher proportion of female children than male children survives (as was pointed out in the case of infant mortality rates). Secondly, rural child mortality exceeded urban child mortality. In other words, children born in the urban areas of Papua New Guinea have a slightly better chance of survival than children in the rural areas. The rural–

Table 6.11A: Estimates of the reference period t(x)ª, to which the estimated probabilities of dying refer, West model (rural and urban): Papua New Guinea 1979–80

Age group	Age (x)	Parameter estimate	Reference period, $t(x)^a$		
			Males	Females	Both sexes
Rural areas					
15–19	1	q(1)	0.81	0.81	0.81
20–24	2	q(2)	2.13	2.13	2.29
25–29	3	q(3)	4.09	4.07	4.08
30–34	5	q(5)	6.55	6.51	6.53
35–39	10	q(10)	9.30	9.24	9.27
40–44	15	q(15)	12.20	12.12	12.15
45–49	20	q(20)	15.17	15.10	15.14
Urban areas					
15–19	1	q(1)	0.72	0.74	0.73
20–24	2	q(2)	2.09	2.09	2.09
25–29	3	q(3)	4.17	4.14	4.15
30–34	5	q(5)	6.76	6.71	6.74
35–39	10	q(10)	9.66	9.58	9.62
40–44	15	q(15)	12.67	12.56	12.62
45–49	20	q(20)	15.66	15.55	15.60
All sectors					
15–19	1	q(1)	0.77	0.78	0.78
20–24	2	q(2)	2.10	2.10	2.10
25–29	3	q(3)	4.08	4.06	4.07
30–34	5	q(5)	6.58	6.54	6.56
35–39	10	q(10)	9.37	9.30	9.34
40–44	15	q(15)	12.30	12.21	12.26
45–49	20	q(20)	15.29	15.20	15.25

Note: a. Number of years prior to the survey.

urban differential is very pronounced for the $_1q_0$ estimates (where the rural estimates are about twice those estimated for the urban areas). Thirdly, there are some substantial regional differences in child mortality. According to estimates in this survey, child mortality appears to be worse in the New Guinea Mainland and the Highlands regions than in the Papua and New Guinea Islands regions. The New Guinea Islands region has the lowest child-mortality levels out of the four regions. Again, as in the case of infant mortality, the New Guinea Islands region exhibits lower child-mortality levels than those for the urban areas except for the $_1q_0$ estimates. The Papua region occupies a position between the New Guinea Islands region and the New Guinea Mainland and the Highlands regions.

One possible interpretation of the rural–urban and regional differentials might be that as social and economic developments proceed, certain groups and regions receive the benefits of improved education, housing, sanitation and public health before other groups or areas. Thus the urban areas and the New

Table 6.11B: Estimates of the reference period t(x)[a], to which the estimated probabilities of dying refer, West model (regional): Papua New Guinea 1979–80

Age group	Age (x)	Parameter estimate	Reference period, t(x)[a]		
			Males	Females	Both sexes
		Papua Region			
15–19	1	q(1)	0.78	0.79	0.79
20–24	2	q(2)	2.07	2.07	2.07
25–29	3	q(3)	4.12	4.10	4.11
30–34	5	q(5)	6.63	6.60	6.61
35–39	10	q(10)	9.42	9.37	9.40
40–44	15	q(15)	12.35	12.29	12.32
45–49	20	q(20)	15.33	15.28	15.31
		Highlands Region			
15–19	1	q(1)	0.73	0.74	0.74
20–24	2	q(2)	2.05	2.05	2.05
25–29	3	q(3)	4.20	4.17	4.19
30–34	5	q(5)	6.81	6.77	6.79
35–39	10	q(10)	9.72	9.66	9.69
40–44	15	q(15)	12.74	12.65	12.70
45–49	20	q(20)	15.72	15.64	16.68
		New Guinea Mainland Region			
15–19	1	q(1)	0.85	0.85	0.85
20–24	2	q(2)	2.04	2.04	2.04
25–29	3	q(3)	3.91	3.89	3.90
30–34	5	q(5)	6.20	6.17	6.19
35–39	10	q(10)	8.77	8.73	8.75
40–44	15	q(15)	11.55	11.50	11.53
45–49	20	q(20)	14.54	14.51	15.53
		New Guinea Islands Region			
15–19	1	q(1)	0.74	0.74	0.74
20–24	2	q(2)	2.06	2.06	2.06
25–29	3	q(3)	4.19	4.17	4.18
30–34	5	q(5)	6.79	6.76	6.78
35–39	10	q(10)	9.69	9.64	9.67
40–44	15	q(15)	12.69	12.63	12.66
45–49	20	q(20)	15.67	15.61	15.64

Note: a. Number of years prior to the survey.

Guinea Islands region appear to benefit more than the rural areas and the other three regions. According to this view, differentials could be expected to widen before they would eventually narrow as a result of more widespread diffusion of the benefits of education, public health, better nutrition and better housing and sanitation. While this is quite plausible, it must be noted that the differentials themselves may be changed for reasons quite independent of such a process. For

Table 6.12A: Mortality levels in the West model life tables consistent with the childhood-mortality estimates, q(x), (rural–urban): Papua New Guinea 1979–80

Age x	Rural				Urban				All Sectors			
	Males		Females		Males		Females		Males		Females	
	West Mort. Level	Ref. Date	West Mort. Level	Ref. Date	West Mort. Level	Ref. Date	West Mort. Level	Ref. Date	West Mort. Level	Ref. Date	West Mort. Level	Ref. Date
1	13.3	1978.2	12.4	1978.2	18.5	1978.3	17.0	1978.3	14.8	1978.2	15.8	1978.2
2	15.3	1976.9	14.8	1976.9	15.8	1976.9	15.2	1976.9	15.3	1976.9	15.3	1976.9
3	14.6	1974.9	14.4	1974.9	15.4	1974.8	14.7	1974.9	15.2	1974.9	14.6	1974.9
5	14.6	1972.5	14.3	1972.5	14.8	1972.2	14.4	1972.3	14.7	1972.4	14.4	1972.5
10	14.2	1969.7	13.7	1969.8	15.0	1969.3	14.4	1969.4	14.3	1969.6	14.2	1969.7
15	13.7	1966.8	13.3	1966.9	14.5	1966.3	14.1	1966.4	14.1	1966.7	13.6	1966.8
20	13.1	1963.8	13.1	1963.9	13.5	1963.3	13.5	1963.4	13.3	1963.7	13.3	1963.8

Table 6.12B: Mortality levels in the West model life tables consistent with the childhood-mortality estimates, q(x), (regional): Papua New Guinea 1979–80

Papua Region

Age (x)	Males		Females	
	Mortality Level	Reference Date	Mortality Level	Reference Date
1	15.1	1978.2	16.0	1978.2
2	15.6	1976.9	15.0	1976.9
3	15.4	1974.9	14.6	1974.9
5	15.1	1972.4	14.3	1972.4
10	14.7	1969.6	14.1	1969.6
15	14.5	1966.6	13.9	1966.6
20	13.4	1963.7	13.4	1963.7

Highlands Region

Age (x)	Males		Females	
	Mortality Level	Reference Date	Mortality Level	Reference Date
1	15.2	1978.3	13.4	1978.3
2	15.3	1976.9	14.7	1976.9
3	15.2	1974.8	14.4	1974.8
5	14.5	1972.2	14.1	1972.2
10	14.3	1969.3	13.7	1969.3
15	13.7	1966.3	13.3	1966.3
20	12.8	1963.3	12.8	1963.4

New Guinea Mainland Region

Age (x)	Males		Females	
	Mortality Level	Reference Date	Mortality Level	Reference Date
1	14.9	1978.1	14.3	1978.1
2	15.3	1977.0	15.2	1977.0
3	15.1	1975.1	14.4	1975.1
5	14.3	1972.8	14.1	1972.8
10	14.3	1970.2	13.4	1970.2
15	13.7	1967.4	13.3	1967.4
20	12.7	1964.5	12.8	1964.5

New Guinea Islands Region

Age (x)	Males		Females	
	Mortality Level	Reference Date	Mortality Level	Reference Date
1	16.1	1978.3	15.7	1978.3
2	16.0	1976.9	15.4	1976.9
3	15.4	1974.8	14.7	1974.8
5	15.2	1972.2	14.7	1972.2
10	15.1	1969.3	14.5	1969.4
15	14.9	1966.3	14.4	1966.4
20	14.3	1863.3	14.2	1963.4

example, selective rural–urban migration may attract the more educated with lower child-mortality rates to the larger urban areas like Port Moresby and Lae and thus lower child-mortality rates in these urban areas at the expense of those in rural areas.

6.5 SUMMARY AND CONCLUSION

More recent evidence concerning the crude death rate and infant and child mortality from our survey points to a continuation of the decline in mortality rates which according to Van de Kaa (1971) began in 1946. The estimates of the levels of both infant and child mortality have shown a substantial decline since 1966. This decline is attributed to improvements in public health and medical services and such factors as education and general social and economic development.

All the data concerned with mortality rates (crude death rates, infant mortality and child-mortality rates) reveal that males are more vulnerable than females. This finding confirms the shift from higher to lower mortality levels for females which was first observed in the analysis of the data in the 1971 census. The sex differential in mortality, although not very pronounced, holds for rural–urban residence as well as for the regions. Mortality is also found to be slightly lower in urban areas than in the rural areas — a fact that may be attributed to the availability and easy access to better health services in the urban areas. Regional differentials are more pronounced compared to the rural–urban differentials. The New Guinea Islands region stands out clearly as a region of lower mortality even when compared with mortality rates in urban areas. It is possible that a disproportionate share of the benefits of social and economic development may have gone to the New Guinea Islands region.

Useful information (data) has been collected of a type that could be potentially useful to health planners and policy makers in general in targeting particular areas or age groups for further research and action over health. Also, to the extent that the level of mortality is a health/development indicator, then differential mortality and its changes over time might facilitate the assessment of the achievement of the health services and the provision of general 'basic needs' during the development process.

7

Family Size and Family Planning[1]

7.1 INTRODUCTION

In this chapter some of the economic, socio-cultural, demographic and political factors which influence the use of family-planning methods in the rural and urban areas of Papua New Guinea are described and explored in detail. It is not possible to attempt an analysis of all the variables here, but several of the more important variables that affect the use of modern contraceptive methods will be examined to provide the reader with a certain understanding of the Papua New Guinean society. It is also anticipated that the results will provide a framework for policy formulation and implementation.

There are obvious differences in the levels of education and income between the rural and urban sectors of the country, for example, a large number of the urban male respondents are educated above the primary level and are therefore engaged in employment with greater remuneration than their rural counterparts. However, awareness and attitudes to and the practice of contraception were not significantly different in the urban areas from those in the rural areas.

7.2 ATTITUDES TO FAMILY SIZE

The rural and urban respondents have similar views about the ideal number of children. The rural respondents indicated that the ideal size for a rural family should be six children (a mean of 6.0 from male respondents and 6.2 from female respondents) but the urban respondents indicated that the ideal number of children in a family should be four (means of 3.8 and 3.9). The urban respondents also indicated by their responses that four children (means of 3.7 and 3.8) was considered to be ideal for an urban family and six (means 6.3 and

---

1. A condensed form of this chapter has been published in the Journal of Bio-social Science. Vol. 16 No. 3, 1984, and it is reproduced here (with some additional material) with the kind permission of the Galton Foundation.

Table 7.1: Percentage distribution of respondents' opinion on advantages and disadvantages of small and large families: Papua New Guinea

Advantages

Small family	Rural		Urban	
	Males	Females	Males	Females
None	77.0	5.3	70.9	6.9
Enough land	2.1	21.4	1.4	18.6
Enough money	4.3	9.7	5.3	11.0
Enough food and clothing	3.4	38.4	6.5	42.8
Able to educate children	6.6	2.7	9.1	4.8
Less family problems (financial, health etc.)	1.9	7.0	1.6	5.4
Other	3.4	5.0	2.6	3.9
Don't know	0.2	6.3	0.5	2.1
Omitted	1.1	4.2	2.1	4.5
Total	100.0	100.0	100.0	100.0

Large family	Rural		Urban	
	Males	Females	Males	Females
None	0.7	4.9	1.3	8.4
Help with housework	3.1	6.2	2.8	3.5
Help in the farm (garden)	1.9	1.7	2.2	3.7
Support in old age	33.3	18.5	35.7	20.3
Happier family	16.9	19.4	12.9	17.3
Financial advantage	22.5	25.6	19.3	28.1
Status strength of clan	17.8	18.1	20.1	14.3
Other	1.7	2.2	1.2	0.6
Don't know	1.1	1.6	1.8	2.9
Omitted	1.0	1.8	2.7	0.9
Total	100.0	100.0	100.0	100.0

Disadvantages

Small family	Rural		Urban	
	Males	Females	Males	Females
None	6.4	9.1	11.8	16.2
No support in old age	46.7	33.6	40.6	30.7
Parents might be left with no children (death)	21.8	19.3	15.0	14.8
Unhappy family	9.7	13.5	11.2	9.5
Children spoiled	4.6	6.5	5.3	4.3
Other	3.8	2.9	4.2	9.5
Don't know	2.1	9.1	6.5	7.8
Omitted	4.9	6.0	5.4	7.2
Total	100.0	100.0	100.0	100.0
Number of respondents	1066	1857	1231	2129

Large family	Rural		Urban	
	Males	Females	Males	Females
None	83.0	5.3	78.3	7.2
Land shortage	2.6	27.3	1.6	19.9
Unable to educate children	6.0	17.8	7.7	25.6
Financial problems	2.1	14.1	1.1	24.8
Less food, clothing, etc.	1.5	8.7	0.4	6.2
Health and other family problems	0.2	7.9	2.8	3.8
Other	2.3	4.9	2.8	3.3
Don't know	0.8	7.6	1.4	4.2
Omitted	2.0	6.4	3.9	4.8
Total	100.0	100.0	100.0	100.0
Number of respondents	1066	1857	1231	2129

6.1) for a rural family. The respondents were also asked how many children make up a small or a big family. Approximately 80 per cent of both the rural and urban respondents considered four or fewer children to be a small family and six or more to be a big family. When asked if they favoured having a large family, 91 per cent of the male respondents and 85.3 per cent of the female rural respondents and 72.2 per cent and 64.4 per cent respectively of the male and female urban respondents answered affirmatively.

The respondents were asked about the advantages and disadvantages of having small and large families (see Table 7.1). Four main reasons for favouring a large family were: (1) support in old age; (2) the family would be happier; (3) financial advantages — more children would bring in more income; (4) the clan/family has status and strength. However, the female respondents considered the following to be disadvantages of having a large family: (1) the shortage of land; (2) the inability to educate all the children; (3) financial problems. The majority of the male respondents did not think there were any disadvantages in having a large family. Approximately 70 per cent of the rural females and 72.4 per cent of the urban female respondents thought that (1) enough land; (2) enough money; (3) enough food and clothing to be the advantages of having a small family. Again, in contrast, the majority of male respondents thought that there were no advantages in having a small family. The main disadvantages of having a small family given by the respondents was that there would be lack of support in old age and that the children might predecease their parents, leaving them destitute in old age (see Table 7.1).

7.3 KNOWLEDGE AND USE OF CONTRACEPTION

Tables 7.2A and 7.2B give the percentage distribution of the awareness, usage, current usage or ignorance of both modern and traditional methods of contraception. There was overall awareness of some form of contraception in the majority of the respondents, the average per method being 42.1 per cent and 45.6 per cent of the rural male and female respondents, and 51 per cent and 56 per cent of the urban males and females. However, the levels of overall usage, both previous and current are low compared with the level of awareness, and only a small proportion of those who know of a method of contraception actually practise it.

The most well-known methods of contraception in both urban and rural areas are village medicine, breastfeeding, the pill, the injection and sexual abstinence. The traditional methods of breastfeeding, sexual abstinence and village medicine are the most commonly used methods and in current use by people in rural areas. In the urban areas, the most commonly used contraceptives include the pill, the injection (Depo-provera) and the ovulation/rhythm method as well as traditional methods. Current usage of modern contraceptive methods is relatively low compared with breastfeeding and sexual abstinence in both the rural and the

Table 7.2A: Percentage distribution of rural male and female respondents knowing, using and having no knowledge of contraceptive methods: Papua New Guinea

| Method | Awareness | | Knowledge and usage | | | | | | | |
| | | | Usage | | Current usage | | No knowledge | | Omitted | |
	Males	Females	Males	Females	Males	Females	Males	Females	Males	Females
aVillage medicine	59.0	59.9	15.7	13.1	8.8	6.9	37.9	38.9	3.2	1.2
aBreastfeeding	59.4	60.6	38.1	32.2	28.2	23.5	33.6	37.2	7.0	2.2
Pill	48.4	55.7	9.5	7.7	6.7	4.2	45.2	42.4	6.4	1.7
Injection	43.6	52.9	8.0	5.1	5.4	7.1	49.7	45.1	6.7	2.0
Loop	33.9	48.3	1.9	3.2	1.6	1.8	59.0	49.4	7.1	2.3
Condom	35.6	34.1	2.2	0.2	1.3	0.0	58.0	61.0	6.4	4.9
Ovulation/rhythm	29.4	33.6	8.0	7.2	5.9	5.0	63.0	63.1	7.6	3.3
aWithdrawal	23.3	21.5	3.8	2.0	2.7	1.4	69.6	73.3	7.1	5.2
aAbstention	46.6	44.4	29.1	21.2	22.1	16.5	46.2	51.2	7.2	4.4
Number of cases	1066	1857								

Note: a. Traditional contraceptive methods

Table 7.2B: Percentage distribution of urban male and female respondents knowing, using and having no knowledge of contraceptive methods: Papua New Guinea

					Knowledge and usage					
	Awareness		Usage		Current usage		No knowledge		Omitted	
Method	Males	Females	Males	Females	Males	Females	Males	Females	Males	Females
aVillage medicine	52.8	64.5	8.9	10.8	5.7	5.4	42.7	33.9	4.5	1.6
aBreastfeeding	51.5	53.5	28.4	24.6	22.6	16.4	41.4	43.3	7.1	3.2
Pill	59.8	75.0	12.7	19.7	8.9	10.5	40.2	23.0	0.0	2.0
Injection	54.4	70.3	8.9	11.9	6.0	7.1	40.1	27.4	5.5	2.3
Loop	51.9	68.2	5.7	5.5	3.9	2.5	42.4	29.2	5.7	2.6
Condom	58.4	52.8	7.2	1.9	4.3	0.7	35.5	42.1	6.1	5.1
Ovulation/rhythm	45.5	46.2	12.9	11.1	10.0	7.4	47.1	50.2	7.4	3.6
aWithdrawal	33.0	27.8	6.5	5.2	5.6	2.9	58.1	66.2	25.1	6.0
aAbstention	47.3	45.7	19.8	18.9	15.6	12.9	43.7	47.8	9.0	6.5
Number of cases	1231	2129								

Note: a. Traditional contraceptive methods.

urban areas. However, in rural areas 20.9 per cent of the wives of male respondents and 18.1 per cent of the female respondents are using one or other of the non-traditional methods; in urban areas the proportions are 33.1 and 28.2 per cent respectively. The most popular methods are the pill, the injection (Depo-provera) and the ovulation/rhythm method (see Tables 7.2A and 7.2B).

Breastfeeding and sexual abstinence feature significantly in terms of always being used both in the past and in the present in both rural and urban areas. However, the figures for urban areas are between 5 and 10 per cent lower than those for rural areas. This is probably because access to modern contraceptives is easier in urban areas.

The respondents were asked which method they would use to space the number of children they wished to have. Interestingly enough, only a little over 1 per cent of both the rural and urban male respondents and approximately 3 per cent of the rural and urban female respondents indicated that they would use breastfeeding. This probably reveals the lack of knowledge about the inhibiting effect of breastfeeding on fertility. Alternatively, perhaps, due to perceived risk, breastfeeding is not given as a preferred method. Sexual abstinence is by far the most common method that is used (51.7 per cent of the rural males, 39.2 per cent of the rural females, 30.7 per cent of urban males and 18.3 per cent of urban females), followed by 'family planning'. The answer 'family planning' is used by the respondents to cover the whole range of modern contraceptives. The term is used when the respondents cannot think of a particular contraceptive to be used over the long-term, have no particular preference or have not yet been to the family-planning clinic but intend to go when they have all the children they want.

The survey revealed that in rural areas the wives of the male respondents and the female respondents currently practising contraception obtained their supplies from the aid posts, family-planning clinics and hospitals. In urban areas the majority (93 per cent) obtained their supplies from the family-planning clinics and hospitals. The remaining 7 per cent, who obtained their supplies privately from doctors, were probably single women who could not obtain contraceptives from the clinics or hospitals because without a husband to sign a consent form, a woman cannot be issued with contraceptives.

7.3.1 Sterilisation

Thirteen (four rural and nine urban) of the female respondents that were interviewed had been sterilised (representing 0.2 per cent and 0.4 per cent). Interestingly, none of the male respondents had had a vasectomy. When respondents were asked if they had heard of a special operation called sterilisation that stops men and women from having children, 28 per cent of rural males and 36.4 per cent of rural females were aware of sterilisation. The corresponding figures for their urban counterparts were approximately 47 per cent and 53 per cent. These respondents were asked whether they would consider being sterilised if they had all the children they wanted. Only about 11 per cent of rural males, 23 per cent of rural females, 18 per cent of urban males and 34.6 per cent of urban females said that they would consider it in that situation. Among those who would not consider it, about 70 per cent each of rural males and females, 53 per cent of urban males and 64.2 per cent of urban females said that they feared side effects from the operation. Twenty-two per cent of rural males and 26 per cent of rural females, 38 per cent of urban males and 29.8 per cent of the urban females said that they feared the operation, whilst 8 per cent of rural males, 4 per cent of rural females, 9 per cent of urban males and 6 per cent of urban females indicated that they might want more children in the future.

7.3.2 Attitudes to modern contraception

The attitudes of urban male and female respondents to the use of modern contraceptives were similar to those of their rural counterparts. When asked why they were not using these methods, the most frequently stated reason given by 81 per cent of rural males and 76 per cent of urban males was the possible danger to the health of the woman and to future offspring. Other reasons were disapproval by the husband (68 per cent of rural females and 59.5 per cent of urban females), the desire for more children, etc.

7.3.3 Non-users of contraception

Table 7.3 shows that of people not using a method of contraception, 27.7 per cent of rural males and 36.8 per cent of rural female respondents would use contraceptives if they were available, but 42.1 per cent of rural males and 35.9 per cent of rural females would not even if they were available. The figures for the urban non-users of contraceptives include 32.1 per cent of males and 37.4 per cent of females who would use contraceptives if they were available. These figures do not differ significantly from those of the rural non-users. Twenty-five per cent of urban males and 22.3 per cent of urban females would not use contraceptives even if they were available! It is interesting to note that these figures are considerably lower than those for the rural respondents. The figures for the 'don't know', 'would not use' and 'no response' (particularly among the urban respondents) in Table 7.3 are questionable. This is because either the respondents or the interviewers may not consider sexual abstinence as a valid form of contraception. It is therefore possible that the high percentage of respondents who consider themselves to have no knowledge of or to be non-users of contraception, have in fact used and will continue to use sexual abstinence at certain times, but have no knowledge of and/or would not use any modern methods of contraception.

Table 7.3: Percentage distribution of non-users amongst both rural and urban respondents who would use and would not use contraceptives if available: Papua New Guinea

Non-users	Rural respondents		Urban respondents	
	Male	Female	Male	Female
Would use	27.7	36.8	32.1	37.4
Would not use	42.1	35.9	25.0	22.3
Don't know	0.2	0.9	0.2	0.8
Not applicable	13.8	14.3	15.8	7.3
No response	4.3	1.2	11.5	21.7
Omitted	11.9	10.9	15.4	10.5
Total	100.0	100.0	100.0	100.0
Total number of respondents	1066	1857	1231	2129
Number of non-users	831	1523	960	1486

7.3.4 Sources of information about contraception

The primary sources of information are through contact with the health services (see Table 7.4) and relatives. Friends and the schools also provide certain information, the latter in particular for the male respondents. The mass media seems to have little impact (except among the urban males) as a source of information.

Table 7.4: Percentage distribution of sources of information about contraceptives among rural and urban respondents: Papua New Guinea

Sources of information	Rural		Urban	
	Males	Females	Males	Females
Radio	5.8	4.3	7.7	4.6
Newspapers/magazines	4.9	1.4	6.5	2.0
Church	2.2	1.2	2.5	2.2
Friends	8.0	13.1	8.5	7.7
Clinic/hospital	36.7	48.3	39.8	54.4
Relatives	25.7	20.2	23.9	17.4
School	7.3	2.9	8.6	3.2
Omitted	9.4	8.6	2.5	8.5
Total	100.0	100.0	100.0	100.0
Number of respondents[a]	449	847	633	1190

Note: a. Those aware of contraception.

7.3.5 Age at first marriage

Nag (1962) says that rather than the age at first marriage being relevant, the age at which regular sexual union begins is even more so. 'Marriage' in Papua New Guinea may be examined briefly. According to Strathern (1972) it may be difficult to distinguish between casual liaisons and regular unions, and that in Hagen society at least, the major brideprice and gifts are sometimes delayed until the birth of children. It has become acceptable for a man and a woman to live together (especially in urban areas in Papua New Guinea) in a common-law marriage for a period of time before the brideprice payment is exacted from the man or his family. There is no general rule for the whole of Papua New Guinea, especially now that many people are marrying out of their tribal groups and the rules pertaining to this type of situation vary according to, in the main, the acceptability of the man and the woman to each other's family and the community in which they live.

This survey shows that 48.1 per cent of rural males and 51 per cent of the urban males married between the ages of 20 and 24. In fact, 20.1 per cent of rural males and 16.5 per cent of urban males married even earlier, between the ages of 15 and 19. With regard to the female respondents, 49.4 per cent of rural females and 53.9 per cent of the urban females married between the ages of 15 and 19. The mean ages at first marriage for rural males and females are 21.2 years and 17.4 years respectively, whilst for their urban counterparts they are 21.6 and 17.2 years respectively. The urban male and female respondents in the age groups 20–24 and 15–19 (males and females respectively) have a slight edge over their rural counterparts in terms of early marriages. There are three possible explanations for this. Firstly, the sex ratio in the urban centres is significantly imbalanced in favour of males. Because of this, the demand for females is higher than it is in the rural areas and there is greater pressure on the urban females to marry at an earlier age than the rural females. Secondly, common-law marriages are prevalent in the urban centres and there is a greater number of casual liaisons involving young men and women. Thirdly, unless a young woman has some kind of marketable skill, she is considered to be a burden in urban society and there is more pressure on her to marry to protect her reputation, and hopefully to bring an income to her family through the payment of brideprice.

Overall, social experience and accumulated knowledge (especially in a formal sense) before marriage appears to be minimal. Consequently, this not only inhibits communication between husband and wife, but also leaves the young married couple very susceptible to family and/or group pressure with regard to socially acceptable behaviour with regard to childbearing. The fact that the second most common source of family-planning information comes from 'relatives' indicates that there must be some direct or indirect pressure from family members, especially in an extended-family system and social behaviour outside the accepted bounds is likely to lead to disapproval.

The early age at first marriage of the female respondents is especially significant in explaining their attitudes toward contraception. Women in Papua New Guinea are usually under pressure to submit to the demands of men, whether they be husband or father, brother or uncle. And when the women get married, they take on the additional responsibility of 'wife' role required by their husbands and their kin. Because the majority appear to marry young between the ages of 15 and 19 with little knowledge or experience, they would probably think it improper to question, let alone go against traditional norms.

In the rural areas surveyed, most of which have reasonable access to urban centres, it can be assumed that the functional usefulness of sexual abstinence is declining with the gradual input of Western values. Unless there is a very active family-planning programme, people will not be encouraged to accept modern family-planning metods, but will be encouraged to bear children earlier in marriage or even before marriage.

Although there is easier access to information about family planning in urban areas, the youthfulness of the females at first marriage inhibits them in many instances, from using some of these facilities. Besides, the conservative attitudes of many husbands with regard to the sort of behaviour appropriate for their wives and the sort of influences they should be subjected to, leaves young wives isolated from a network of communication, most of their contacts being with relatives or alternatively, 'wantoks' (people from the same cultural background, language group or even district) both of which may be members of the same household or may live in the same town.

7.3.6 Education and income

The selected socio-economic characteristics reveal that both the levels of education and income of both the rural and the urban respondents in this survey are very low. About 69 per cent of rural males, 45 per cent of urban males, approximately 79 per cent of rural females and 68 per cent of urban females have had no education or just primary education. Approximately 15 per cent of rural males and 47 per cent of urban males, 7.4 per cent of rural females and 25 per cent of urban females have gone beyond the primary level (see Tables 3.1A and 3.1B). It therefore follows that the occupations of most of the respondents are those that do not require skills. The monthly income for the majority is not more than K100.0.

Education is important in determining attitudes towards and the practice of family planning. Several studies show that women who have received some education (particularly to high-school level and above) know more about and also practise family planning in contrast to women with no education. For example, in a recent survey comparing the attitudes of Papua New Guinea with Australian high-school students towards family size and contraception show that Papua New Guinean high-school male students preferred large families — nearly half of them wanted four children or more. The Australian male and female students and the Papua New Guinean female students held similar views about the size of their intended families. The female students in Papua New Guinea also had a knowledge of contraception that was equivalent to that of the Australian students, whereas their male counterparts who wanted more children also knew less about contraception. It appears that education and the family-planning activities in Papua New Guinea are making the students more aware of modern contraception (Callan and Wilks, 1982).

Data from this survey reveal that women with no education and women with some education (particularly to the primary level) know as much and have similar attitudes towards the practice of family-planning methods. This is supported by the fact that information about family planning at school begins either during the last year of primary school (Standard 6) or at high school. It is evident that many of our female respondents have not reached this level. Also, the average age of the rural and urban female respondents is 30.5 and 26.7 respectively, indicating that those women who attended school, did so at a time when the education of women was considered to be even less important than it is now. Many more women then would have been under considerable pressure from their fathers (and many still are) regarding the unimportance of their education, especially higher education, as opposed to the traditional role of women. A common opinion in Papua New Guinea, especially among men with little or no education, is that 'women get too many ideas through school and do not make good wives', they are not as pliable to traditional customs.

The husband's educational level is also an important factor (for the same reason as it is for the women) with regard to knowledge about, attitudes towards, and the practice of family planning. Our data show that approximately 36 per cent of the husbands of rural females and 11 per cent of those of urban females have no education. Also, about 25 per cent and 29 per cent of the husbands of rural and the urban female respondents have been educated to the primary level only. Even though more than 16 per cent of the rural husbands and 40 per cent of the urban husbands have some secondary and tertiary education, most of the husbands have a negative attitude towards the use of modern contraception. It is the husband's attitude, because he has to sign the consent form, that governs whether or not his wife will use modern contraception.

With regard to income, it is significant to note that approximately 17 per cent of the rural males and 9 per cent of the husbands of the rural females earn between K100.00 and K299.00 per month. On the other hand, approximately 73 per cent of the urban males and 55 per cent of the husbands of the urban females earn between K100.00 and K299.00 per month (the average for unskilled/semi-skilled workers in Papua New Guinea). Although the income levels for the urban respondents are higher than they are for the rural respondents, they are low by general wage levels in Papua New Guinea. This factor is important with regard to individual incentives to use modern contraception. It is not uncommon for whole families (both nuclear and extended) to be supported on wages such as those reported by the respondents, with little extra help from the 'wantok system'. Under the circumstances, the purchase of contraceptives is, in many instances, considered to be of secondary importance (if it can be afforded — supplies carry a charge which ranges from about 7 US cents per condom to about 7 US dollars for Depo-provera injections) and the primary needs for food, clothing and shelter take priority.

107

7.3.7 Power structure within the household

As stated in the chapter on breastfeeding and sexual abstinence, the power structure in the household is an important factor when considering decision-making with regard to the use of modern contraception. The role that the husband and the wife play in decision-making is particularly relevant to this subject. Our data show that at least in theory, 63 per cent of rural males, 68 per cent of the rural females, 72 per cent of urban males and approximately 73 per cent of urban females said that both the husband and the wife should acquire information about family planning together. What happens in practice is unknown.

Table 7.5 shows levels of communication between the spouses. The data indicates that although communication with regard to family planning is possible between about 22 per cent of rural males and 28 per cent of rural females and their spouses, actual communication affects only an average of 18.5 per cent of all the rural respondents. The difference in the level between possible and actual communication among the urban male and urban female respondents is not very high. However, 20 per cent of the urban males and approximately 18 per cent of the urban females have no communication with their spouses. The figures for their rural counterparts are 29 per cent of males and 26.4 per cent of females. The most common reason given for lack of communication where possible is 'other'. Because extended families remain prevalent in both rural and urban areas of Papua New Guinea and ethnic groups have the tendency to 'stick together' in new environments, it can be assumed that a large portion of 'other' is the presence of adult members of the family. And because it appears that the use of modern contraceptives is not a pressing subject until the completion of the family to the desired size, its discussion is likely to be disregarded and ultimately, the traditional method of sexual abstinence is fallen back on.

Because men are usuallly head of the household, their approval or disapproval can have a significant effect on the practice of family planning by women. O'Collins (1979) notes from a group discussion in a village in Madang Province, that 'the women were very interested in the spacing of children (by modern methods of contraception), they were not fully informed about the possible methods but they felt if the man approved it would be alright'. She also notes another instance in New Ireland Province where young women were afraid to discuss the subject of contraception in front of older women for fear of disapproval. These two examples point to the lack of power in domestic decision-making that women have in at least two traditional rural societies in Papua New Guinea and it is safe to say that these findings apply to the majority of traditional settings in the country.

It is important to note that the husband's attitude is also subjected to the constant and subtle pressure from other family members. And although husbands may agree that there are benefits to be gained by practising family planning, they may not consider it to be worthwhile if it causes internal family friction.

The educational and socio-economic status of the husband, his knowledge,

Table 7.5: Percentage distribution of level of communication with regard to contraception between spouses for rural and urban respondents: Papua New Guinea

Communication	Rural respondents		Urban respondents	
	Male	Female	Male	Female
Possible	21.7	27.5	29.1	35.3
Actual	16.7	20.3	23.1	28.9
None	29.0	26.4	20.0	17.7
Not applicable	13.8	14.3	15.4	7.3
No response	16.5	7.5	8.8	7.1
Omitted	2.3	4.0	3.6	3.7
Total	100.0	100.0	100.0	100.0
Number of respondents[a]	499	847	633	1190

Note: a. Those aware of contraception.

and the amount of respect he is accorded by other family members is significant in shaping new values and/or modifying old ones. For example, if the 'husband is not the head of the household, but has a high level of education, his opinion may carry more weight, although he and his wife are subjected to the rules set down by the head of the household. If he does not have a high level of education or has not earned the respect of other family members in some other way, he and his wife will be compelled to conform, without question, as long as they are members of that household. If the husband has a high level of education and a high socio-economic status and is the head of the household, he will not only be more aware of the individual benefits of family planning, but will be more able to successfully resist pressure from more conservative members of the family.

The wife, regardless of her educational and socio-economic status is under pressure both from her husband and his/her family to conform to what is deemed socially acceptable behaviour within the household. Although she has some influence over certain decisions, especially concerning children, it is her husband who usually makes the final decision. This decision-making power manifests itself with regard to family planning because the husband must give his written consent before his wife can be issued with any form of modern contraception. The husband's approval (which may or may not be influenced by relatives) would therefore create an artificial barrier to the use of family-planning services.

Another important point with regard to the influence of other family members over the use of modern methods of contraception by a couple, is whether or not the regular practice of coitus is considered to be socially acceptable. In many traditional societies in Papua New Guinea, frequent sexual intercourse between husband and wife is often frowned upon. This is a real deterrent to husbands and wives living in an extended family who therefore do not see the need to use contraceptives while they are subjected to such sexual taboos. Here again, the husband's level of education, especially if he is the head of the household, could give him and his wife greater resistance to family pressure regarding these beliefs.

It is thus evident that whoever wields power in the household has a great deal of influence over the rest of the members, especially with regard to family size. In addition, older members of an extended family also have some influence over the regularity of coitus between husbands and wives, and consequently, the need to use modern contraception.

7.3.8 The ideal number of children

The ideal number of children in the extended family is influenced by the prevailing social and economic values and conditions, the perceived rewards and the cost of bearing children. It is also related to the household and the power structure in the community (especially in rural areas) which can have a drastic effect on the importance married couples put on the serious and continued use of modern contraception in relation to the spacing of births or the limiting of family size. The average ideal number of children for the rural male and female respondents are 6.7 and 6.2 children respectively, indicating a preference for large families. The corresponding figures in urban areas are 3.7 and 3.8 children, indicating a change to a preference for families of medium size. When compared with the average number of living children (3.7 and 3.6 for the rural male and female respondents respectively and 2.5 and 2.3 for their urban counterparts) it is apparent that these respondents would probably exceed their ideal family size in the absence of family planning. It is particularly interesting that at least 2 per cent and 1 per cent of urban male and female respondents did not want children.

7.3.9 The desire for more children

In response to the question, 'Would you like more, less or the same number of children as you already have?', the data from rural areas show that approximately 33 per cent of males and 39 per cent of females are satisfied with their present number of children and that 17 per cent of the male and 16 per cent of the female respondents wanted more children. Only 5 per cent of males and 6 per cent of female respondents wanted fewer children than they already had. The urban data show that approximately 18 per cent of males and 22 per cent of females wanted more children, 23.4 per cent of males and 30.6 per cent of females were satisfied with their present number of children and only about 5 per cent of each sex wanted fewer. However, a large number of people from both rural and urban areas were non-committal. There are differences in the desire for more children between rural and urban areas, but the information collected indicates the need for a more serious family-planning campaign in both areas.

Related to the desire for more children is the question of the preferred sex for the additional children — 'Would you prefer to have more daughters or more sons?' The data from the rural areas show that about 23 per cent of males and 13 per cent of females preferred male children, whilst 3.3 per cent of males and 12.4 per cent of females preferred female children. About a third of all respondents said they had no special preference and about 19 per cent of males and 23 per cent of females were in the 'don't know' category and would possibly be happy with either sex. The urban data show that approximately 20 per cent of males and 12 per cent of females preferred male children, 2.2 per cent and 11 per cent of the male and female respondents respectively preferred male children, 30.4 per cent of males and 38.2 per cent of females would be happy with either and about 23 per cent of males and 19 per cent of females were in the 'don't know' category.

Fawcett (1977) made the interesting observation that 'a general value system can . . . have an important influence on the perceived value of children and in some circumstances can carry greater weight than the more immediate economic and social factors affecting the family'. The perceived value of children is evident from the data. Approximately 87 per cent of rural males and 91 per cent of rural females expected financial support in their old age from their children whilst for their urban counterparts the figures are 88 per cent and 91 per cent for the male and female respondents respectively. Both the rural and the urban figures are similar and emphasise the continuing importance of the extended family in providing some form of social security for its members in both the rural and urban areas of Papua New Guinea. It appears therefore that those respondents who opted for sons did so mainly because they believe their sons can earn money and would be more able to give them ongoing physical and financial support in their old age, than would their daughters. Many of those who opted for daughters did so because of their daughters' expected brideprice. Because of this overall positive attitude with regard to the future services of both sons and daughters, it is favourable to most respondents to have an equal number of either sex.

The casual use of contraception can thus be related to the desire for an additional child of a particular sex to conform with individual perception of an ideal family size. Until this is achieved, there appears to be no continued use of contraception other than breastfeeding and sexual abstinence. The data reveal that although a slightly higher proportion of respondents have used methods like village medicine, the pill, injection and the ovulation method especially after the first birth, there is no single modern method that is used by both rural and the urban respondents.

7.3.10 Accessibility to family-planning services

Table 7.6 indicates the availability of contraceptives to the respondents. Over half of the rural respondents and over 70 per cent of the urban respondents who were aware of contraception said that contraceptives were available at either the hospital, the clinic or at the aid post (rural areas). But about a quarter of the rural respondents and fewer of the urban respondents (13 per cent of males and 9 per cent of females) said that contraceptives were not available.

Table 7.6: Availability of contraceptives at clinics/hospitals/aid posts — percentage distribution recorded amongst rural and urban respondents: Papua New Guinea

Availability	Rural		Urban	
	Males	Females	Males	Females
Yes	54.5	61.8	72.1	75.9
No	28.2	23.7	13.4	8.9
Don't know	3.7	1.4	3.6	2.8
No response	2.6	3.7	3.0	2.2
Omitted	11.0	9.4	7.9	10.2
Total	100.0	100.0	100.0	100.0
Number of respondents[a]	449	847	633	1190

Note: a. Those aware of contraception.

There is a vast difference between awareness of contraceptives and their use in both rural and urban areas as indicated in Tables 7.2A and 7.2B. The data imply that if contraceptives are required in the urban areas they can be easily obtained if the husband signs the consent form and if there is enough money to buy them. The instances of reported unavailability of contraceptives in rural areas could be due to the shortage of health personnel in these areas. It may be assumed then, that if people in rural areas have access to provincial hospitals, they are able to obtain contraceptives if they wish. For those who are restricted because of the nature of their work, lack of money to get to the town, etc., reliance on the aid post is useless because in most cases, the aid posts carry only stocks of essential curative medicines. Besides, another inhibiting factor of would-be users of modern contraceptives is that most of the health-extension workers and aid-post orderlies in rural areas are men. In such circumstances, it is very difficult for women who are interested in trying a modern contraceptive to discuss the subject with a man without a great deal of embarrassment.

It appears then, that even though there is physical accessibility to family-planning services for most urban dwellers and about half of the rural population, the problems of non-use are mainly of a sociological and psychological nature as stated earlier. These problems include the attitudes of the husbands to the use of contraception by their wives, the reinforcement of culturally acceptable behaviour by the extended family and the community and the desire for more children. Besides, sexual abstinence is still widespread and is being promoted indirectly by the government's breastfeeding programme introduced in 1977. Sexual abstinence is used effectively to space births both in rural and urban areas and it is not surprising therefore that this survey reveals that modern contraceptives are not used for child spacing by Papua New Guineans.

7.4 SUMMARY AND CONCLUSION

In conclusion, it seems that economic pressures are being felt within the family in both rural and urban areas and that the cost of raising children is clearly perceived, at least among the educated. In spite of this, the majority of Papua New Guineans desire large numbers of children — six or more — the main reason being for economic security in old age. At the present time, there is little evidence to suggest that a change in these attitudes towards a high fertility rate in Papua New Guinea will come soon.

It is also evident that people have a negative attitude towards modern methods of birth control simply because they are ill-informed. The most frequently stated reason, that the effects of using contraceptives harm the health of the mother (the user) and the future offspring, is probably one of the obstacles to their more widespread use. The current policy of the husband signing the consent form is yet another obstacle. Traditionally, fertility control was the affair of women (breastfeeding, sexual abstinence, village medicine, etc.) who now feel that they have no control over their own fertility. In addition, the policy bars single women from participating actively in the family-planning programme.

Other factors include the cost of supplies and the availability of personnel. Contraceptives are expensive and this may serve as an obstacle to their use by poor rural and urban couples. Also, there is a shortage of health workers in some of the rural areas. Even if the rural population has access to provincial hospitals, they are not necessarily able to obtain contraceptives even if they wish to. Those who because of the nature of their work or lack of funds, have restricted access to the hospital cannot rely on the aid posts because, in most cases, these carry only stocks of essential curative medicines. Since most of the health-extension workers and aid-post orderlies in the rural areas are men, it is very difficult for women who are interested in trying modern contraceptive methods to discuss the subject with them.

The problems of non-use are mainly of a more sociological and psychological nature and include the attitudes of the husbands to the use of contraceptives by their wives, the reinforcement of culturally acceptable behaviour by the extended family and the community and the desire for more children.

The fertility level of Papua New Guinean women is high and there is little effort to control it. It is, however, interesting that whereas the majority of the female respondents in both the rural and urban areas see several advantages in

113

having small families and disadvantages to having large ones, the majority of the men think otherwise. Papua New Guinea will probably continue to be characterised as a country with a high level of fertility for some time to come.

Although the levels of awareness about contraceptives are relatively high, the overall impression is that the practice of using modern methods of birth control in both rural and urban areas is low. Despite the rural–urban differences in education levels, and in income, in living conditions and in the availability of family-planning services, awareness and current use is only slightly higher among the urban respondents. Yet in the light of the high levels of fertility in Papua New Guinea and the various obstacles facing the family-planning programme, even the present low level of contraceptive usage might be considerd to represent substantial progress. However, if the family-planning programme is to have a significant impact in reducing the high levels of fertility and hence the high rate of population growth which is close to three per cent per year, then a much more intensive programme of activities is needed in both the rural and urban areas of the country.

8

Concluding Comments and Policy Implications

8.1 THE IMPLICATIONS OF FAMILY-PLANNING PROGRAMMES AND THE DEMOGRAPHIC TRANSITION

The evidence from the Third-World countries suggests that fertility levels are declining in some of them as a result of the introduction of family-planning services where the people are receptive to the idea of using contraceptives to space out births or to prevent unwanted births. In this brief review of the demographic transition in the Third World, it has been shown that high levels of socio-economic development are not a necessary precondition for a decline in the fertility level. What is the implication of this for Third-World countries in their efforts to reduce the rate of population growth in order to achieve some reasonable level of economic development?

First, it must be noted that the impact of family planning and the decline in fertility levels is loosely related to socio-economic development. For example, China, Indonesia, Thailand, etc. have experienced low to moderate socio-economic development and yet are experiencing a significant decline in fertility levels. Besides, the populations of these three countries are overwhelmingly rural and most people are illiterate. In essence, it is evident that a decline in fertility can precede socio-economic development. This provides some hope for a number of Third-World countries which are struggling to reduce their high rates of population growth and simultaneously trying to develop socio-economically, since, according to Coale and Hoover (1958); Coale (1978), success in the reduction of the rate of population growth can facilitate development.

Secondly, there is strong evidence supporting the hypothesis that the intervention of organised family-planning programmes can facilitate the fertility transition in a receptive society. Data from Singapore, China, Thailand, Indonesia, Taiwan, etc. show that the introduction of family-planning services to a population with a high fertility level can promote a more rapid decline in fertility levels in all sectors than would be expected otherwise. Campaigns promoting family planning in terms of information, education and communication have also increased knowledge about the use of contraceptives and encouraged the practice of family planning.

Thirdly, a society with a high level of fertility is not likely to reduce it to a desired level in the absence of a family-planning programme. However, once the idea that the use of contraception can reduce fertility diffuses through a society, the practical use can expand very quickly (if supplies of contraceptives are available). KAP studies in the 1960s and 1970s have revealed high fertility levels in many Third World countries, many of which still lack adequate information about modern contraceptives or the contraceptives are difficult to obtain. Undoubtedly it appears that substantial declines in fertility levels follow the introduction of family-planning programmes.

Fourthly, a decline in the desired size of families may follow an initial decline in fertility levels within the process of socio-economic development. The economic value of children may be reduced and this in turn may result in a further decline in the size of families and hence the fertility level. This is suggested by the studies of Freedman *et al.* (1977) and Knodel and Debavalya (1978). Bumpass (1973) for example, reports that the new contraceptives (the pill, IUD, sterilisation) have resulted in significant proportions of the population believing that the control of fertility levels is complete and unobtrusive. According to Bumpass, childbearing with these more effective contraceptives becomes voluntary in a markedly different way than with traditional contraceptive mthods. Motherhood itself becomes a matter for rational evaluation once control is certain. Cultural values in support of motherhood were once necessary to ensure the survival of the society in terms of a high rate of mortality and also served to rationalise unwanted births that occurred in the absence of complete control of fertility rates. But with new and effective contraceptives ensuring complete control over fertility, the costs as well as the benefits of motherhood are considered, which results in a decline in the desired number of children. This process is likely to occur in a population in which the participation of women in the labour force is high and the opportunity cost of motherhood is also high.

Finally, in order that family planning has an impact on the fertility levels, those organising family-planning programmes in Third-World countries need to examine the successes and failures of some of the well-structured programmes and to adopt policies that will make the fullest use of the services. Programmes need to adopt the multiple-method and multiple-distribution network approach used by China, Singapore, Thailand, etc. It is evident from this report that well-structured family-planning programmes that provide adequate and continuous services to target populations in both rural and urban areas will effect the transition from a high to a low level of fertility.

8.2 SUMMARY AND CONCLUSION

This report presents some of the major findings of a demographic survey — 'A

Study of Fertility, Mortality and Contraceptive Use in Papua New Guinea'. The main objective of the study was to provide information about rates of fertility and infant and child mortality and about awareness, knowledge, attitudes and the practice of contraception among the Papua New Guinean population. This will provide the basis for the formulation and implementation of policy with regard to the numbers of the population.

Whilst this analysis provides some interesting findings, care must be taken, however, in the use of the data. Several methodological and other problems were encountered in the collection of the data. Besides the problems of interviewer bias in the survey, there were the problems of different interpretations of the questions and difficulties arising from the use of the 'pidgin' language from one province to another. Also, there were difficulties in obtaining accurate measurements of, for example, age, income, education, etc. and problems with the validity of the responses. Despite this, the results point to the fact that there is greater need for a substantial family-planning programme in terms of education and services in the rural and urban areas of Papua New Guinea.

The composition of the various households in terms of age and sex confirms that Papua New Guinea has a very young population, a pattern which is characteristic of all Third-World countries. About 41 per cent of the males and 42 per cent of the females enumerated in our sample are under 15 years old. Of the females, 49 per cent are in the childbearing age group — 15 to 49. Demographically, this young population is evidence of a high level of growth in the population in the recent past and the larger numbers of women in the childbearing age-group portends a high fertility level in the foreseeable future.

With regard to the fertility level, several methods of measuring fertility reveal that it is high. For example, in terms of the number of children ever born at the time of the survey (cumulative fertility), the figures in excess of six children for women aged 45 and over and approximately three children for women aged 25 to 29 indicate a pattern of high fertility. Adjusted figures on births in the 12-month period preceding the survey (current fertility) serve to underscore this pattern. Whilst the adjusted total fertility rates are six and approximately seven children for the rural and urban areas respectively.

Other fertility-related factors examined in the survey included breastfeeding and sexual abstinence. In the absence of breastfeeding, ovulation usually begins again within two months of the birth and the woman is able to become pregnant again. Breastfeeding, however, lengthens the period of postpartum amenorrhea because suckling suppresses ovulation. The mean period of breastfeeding (approximately 22 and 21 months for the rural and urban respondents respectively) can be seen as having some effect on the length of time between births. In addition, the traditional practice of sexual abstinence which accompanies breastfeeding in both the rural and urban areas also affects the length of intervals between births.

This survey has also revealed some significant differences in the attitudes and behaviour between rural and urban respondents. Specifically, the rural female

117

respondents have more children, have lost more children, expected more children, and preferred the idea of having more children than their urban counterparts. At the same time, the rural female respondents were less likely to use or approve of modern family-planning techniques, and were more likely to acknowledge the traditional methods of village medicine, breastfeeding and sexual abstinence than were their urban counterparts.

The majority of the respondents in both rural and urban areas want large families. This is evident when their actual fertility level is compared with their responses concerning their ideal family size and the desire for more children. Both the rural and urban female respondents expressed ideal family sizes that are on the average higher than the mean number of living children. It is also important to point out that the ideal size of family for rural and urban male respondents are similar to those of their female counterparts. Accordingly, it seems likely that the female respondents will achieve their ideal size family, judging from the current average size in Papua New Guinea, unless fertility patterns change drastically in the future through the proper and continued use of modern or traditional methods of birth control.

There was an overall awareness of some form of contraception in the majority of the respondents. However, the levels of overall usage, both previous and current are low compared with the levels of awareness, and only a small proportion of those who know of a method actually practise it. The question then becomes, why aren't more women using a method of contraception when they are aware of at least one? Is it simply a question of the possible danger to the health of the mother and the future offspring or does it go beyond that? If the reason is that it is considered to be harmful, then efforts should be made in the family-planning programme to educate people about the economic benefits and benefits to health as well as providing information about possible side effects that may affect only some users. If however, other socio-cultural factors are involved, then a wider programme is necessary, not one that concentrates primarily on providing a family-planning service.

The proportion of female respondents in both the rural and urban areas who are aware of contraception but do not use any method follows a distinctly curvilinear relationship with age: the youngest and oldest female respondents are least likely to be using some method of contraception whilst those in the mid-childbearing age are most likely. On average, younger women who want more children may be less motivated to prevent another pregnancy than older women since they are likely to have fewer children. Nevertheless, these younger respondents who want more children are more likely to use some form of contraception once their families have reached their ideal sizes. On the other hand, those female respondents who are near the end of their reproductive phase may not use contraception because they believe they are no longer fecund.

Although responses to the question about attitudes towards family planning needs to be interpreted with caution, the significant proportion who had a negative attitude suggests that in addition to the family-planning programme

118

efforts should be made to changing attitudes towards the use of contraception. If the current growth rate of the population is to be reduced to a level conducive to both social and economic development, attitudes towards the sizes of families will also have to change and to effect such a change, nationwide education programmes and other measures will be required.

The data concerning fertility and family planning reveal that some of the most important differences are related to where people live. Fertility is slightly higher in the rural areas, and there is some scanty evidence that a decline in fertility is taking place among young, educated, urban respondents, but not among their counterparts in the rural areas. The latter are less knowledgeable about family planning and, more to the point, are much less likely to be practising it. Although the data show that there is need for more effort to be put in the family-planning programme in urban areas, it is in the rural areas, where the vast majority of Papua New Guinean women live that there is the greatest need for such a service.

8.3 IMPLICATIONS FOR POLICY

The Breastfeeding Promotion Programme that was discussed in chapter 4 should be the pivot on which the formulation of policy hinges. This is because the continuity of the practice of any modern method of contraception other than that of sexual abstinence (usually while a woman is lactating) is negligible in either the rural or urban areas. There is, however, a greater experimentation in the use of modern methods to space out births in the urban areas. The ongoing success of the Breastfeeding Promotion Programme in promoting breast milk as the most nutritious infant food can be seen from the figures in Table 4.1, but these figures are in sharp contrast with the general awareness of the contraceptive connotations of breastfeeding while amenorrhea exists (approximately 60 per cent of both rural males and females and 52 and 54 per cent of urban males and females were aware of this). When taking a broad view of the direction of government policy, the influence of such determinants as the regular practices of breastfeeding and sexual abstinence should be seriously considered. (These determinants are listed in points 1 to 6 in section 4.4 of chapter 4.) Such a policy in Papua New Guinea should look to: (1) maintaining the popularity of breastfeeding and (2) promoting alternatives to sexual abstinence as a method of child spacing if, through social change, use of that method is decreasing.

At present, long periods of breastfeeding suit many of the rural and the urban women because of the nature of their occupations — most of them are self-employed. However, when a greater number of women receive higher standards of education and seek white-collar work and will not be able to breastfeed over a long period, then there will be a greater and long-term demand by individuals for alternative methods of contraception apart from sexual abstinence. In the case of women working in offices, stores or factories, it can be assumed that they will breastfeed for about three months or for as long as the duration of their maternity leave.

Increasingly, alternatives to sexual abstinence will be considered necessary because of the breakdown in social and cultural rules and then institutional communication through the Family-Planning Educational Programme will have a much more understandable part to play. Such a programme should not only be aimed at married couples, but also to unmarried adults, entire households or the whole community, emphasising the need for verbal feedback from older people so that they do not feel excluded. This is a difficult task, and requires much sensitivity by nurses or health-extension workers, depending on the particular situation. It requires skill to promote the nutritional benefits of breastfeeding and to indicate its value as a contraceptive while amenorrhea exists and at the same time, to promote alternative methods of contraception to sexual abstinence. Introduction to these new ideas should be carried out in such a way that public consciousness is raised to the long-term individual and social benefits of child spacing and to a financially manageable number of children.

In terms of family planning, the results of the sample survey conducted in some of the rural and urban areas of Papua New Guinea give a broad notion of current knowledge of, attitudes towards and practice of family planning and provides the basis for future formulation of policy for the country. However, to ensure greater accuracy in providing appropriate guidelines for family-planning services in different areas, data should be analysed and interpreted on a microscopic scale.

The data related to awareness of contraceptives and the levels of their overall usage, both previous and current together with ignorance of their existence constitutes an important basis for the formulation of policy as do the data for non-users, who would not use contraceptives even if they were available. As discussed earlier in chapter 7, these non-users may in fact be using breastfeeding or sexual abstinence or both but do not consider these methods to be valid forms of contraception. The Breastfeeding Promotion Programme, although successful in reducing the level of infant deaths, has been instrumental in consolidating the traditional practice of sexual abstinence and effectively obstructing the serious use of modern contraception to space births. The sources of information about contraception and the way in which such information is presented to and interpreted by the recipients is an important area on which to concentrate when formulating policy.

Family-planning programmes directed at educating young people and married couples are inadequate because of the amount of pressure the recipients are subjected to daily by their families or the community to conform to a particular mode of behaviour. It will be necessary for the long-term success of such a programme to include older members of the family or the community. In this way, deviance from what is considered to be socially acceptable behaviour will not be incomprehensible to the older people and therefore less threatening to what they consider to be traditional norms.

120

Single women are disadvantaged if they wish to use modern contraception for various reasons: social prohibitions generating fear of disapproval; the youth of many of them resulting in a certain lack of confidence in approaching the health workers and most important, the restricted or non-issue of contraceptives to unmarried women by the health workers because of the current policy, which bars single women from obtaining contraceptives. In an effort to compensate for these factors, a change of emphasis in policy and education in family planning is desirable, that is, instead of discouraging single women from using contraceptives they should be encouraged to use them.

Further, the promotion of modern family-planning methods to a basically traditional and conservative group is a very sensitive issue and a difficult task. Some of the common reasons for non-use of modern contraceptives apart from the 'desire for another child' are being 'unable to understand methods', to 'see no need to use contraceptives' and 'other' which could be interpreted (as already discussed) as 'fear of side effects' or 'fear of disapproval from family members'. It is therefore imperative for the leader of any group discussion on family planning to bear in mind these reasons for not using contraceptives and to direct his/her argument with regard to benefits for the individual, the group and the country to the older people, relying to some extent on their verbal feedback.

It is important to stress the health aspects of family planning in policy formulation as outlined by the World Bank (1984). It is common knowledge that early and frequent childbearing contributes to the illness and death of children and mothers in the developing countries. Family-planning programmes can prevent some of these problems by four main mechanisms:

(1) Lengthening the interval between pregnancies (child spacing). The interval between pregnancies is an important determinant of survival for both the newborn baby and his or her older sibling. Infants and children at highest risk are those born less than two years apart. This holds even when allowance is made for the order of birth, the mother's age, the mother's education, whether they live in urban or rural areas or the sex of the child. There are two main explanations for the link between mortality and child spacing. The first is that the youngest and next youngest child must compete for the resources of the family and for the attention of the mother. When a woman becomes pregnant again soon after giving birth, the younger child may be prematurely weaned, increasing the risk that he or she will suffer from malnutrition, gastro-intestinal infection, diarrhoea and other illnesses. The second explanation is that a rapid succession of pregnancies weakens the mother and is linked to a low weight at birth in the newborn baby. According to the World Bank report, if births were spaced two to six years apart, infant mortality would decline by an average of 10 per cent and child mortality by 16 per cent.

(2) Preventing births for women aged under 20 and over 34 years of age. In these age groups, women who become pregnant carry a greater risk of illness and death, both for themselves and their children. Infant and maternal mortality are highest among teenage mothers. In Pakistan, for example, babies born to

121

teenage mothers have a 50 per cent greater chance of dying than do those born to mothers aged 20 to 29 years old. Part of the explanation for this is that teenage mothers may not be mature enough physically for a safe pregnancy; in addition, most of their births are first births, which often carry a higher risk of death for the mother and child. As for mothers over 35 years old, their babies run an increased risk of congenital defects such as Down's Syndrome, cleft palate and certain heart disorders. Infant and maternal mortality also increase for mothers in their 30s and 40s.

(3) Because most births are largely to women in the age group 20 to 34, confining all births to that group would have only a modest effect on overall infant and child mortality rates. For example, birth rates would decline by only 2 to 6 per cent in Indonesia, Pakistan and the Philippines. The effect on maternal mortality is potentially greater.

(4) Allowing couples to have fewer children. Depending on the country, the risks of infant and maternal mortality increase rapidly after the third, fourth or fifth child. In El Salvador for example, infant mortality for the fifth and later children is more than twice the level for the second and third child. In Matlab Thana, Bangladesh, maternal mortality is about 250 per 100,000 live births for the second and third births but is about 450 per 100,000 for the fourth and fifth births. This is true even when allowance is made for differences in the ages of the mothers. If all births of fourth and later children were prevented, infant mortality would decline by between 5 and 11 per cent in Indonesia, Pakistan, the Philippines and Sri Lanka.

Finally, a government policy concerning the growth rate in the population that embraces the three basic demographic variables of fertility, mortality and migration is different from public support for family-planning services. Family-planning programmes provide information and services to help people achieve their own fertility objectives. In contrast, population policy involves explicit demographic goals. It employs a wide range of policies, both direct and indirect, to change the levels of the three basic demographic variables. An effective population policy requires the joint efforts of all governmental and non-governmental agencies working together to achieve overall development objectives for the given national interests. Above all, it requires clear direction and support from the most senior levels of government.

Bibliography

Agyei, W.K.A. (1982a) 'Urban growth problems in Papua New Guinea'. *Pacific Perspective, Journal of the South Pacific Social Sciences Association*, 10(2): 22–30

———— (1982b) *Evaluation of the quality of the demographic data in the population of Papua New Guinea*. ESCAP/SPC Country Monograph Series. United Nations, New York

———— (1979) 'Method of fertility estimation'. In R. Skeldon *et al.* (ed.), *The Demography of Papua New Guinea*. Monograph 11. Institute of Applied Social and Economic Research, Boroko

———— (1978) 'Modernization and the theory of demographic transition in the developing countries: The case of Jamaica'. *Social and Economic Studies*, 27(1): 44–68

Bakker, M.L. (n.d.) *Working Paper No. 7 — Preliminary Fertility Estimates derived from 1980 Census data for Geographical Subdivisions of Papua New Guinea*

———— (1983) *Working Paper No. 4. Spatial Differentiation of Mortality in PNG. A Classification based on the results of the 1980 Census*

Baer, E.C. (1981) 'Promoting breastfeeding: A national responsibility'. *Studies in Family Planning*, 12(4): 198–206

Beaver, S.E. (1975) *Demographic Transition Theory Reinterpreted*. D.C. Heath and Company, Lexington

Bellamy, R.L. (1926) *Enquiry into Vital Statistics of the Trobriand Group*. Papuan Government Report

Biddulph, J. (1980) 'Impact of legislation restricting the availability of feeding bottles in PNG'. *Nutrition and Development*, 3(2): 4–8

Bogue, D.J. (1969) *Principles of Demography*. John Wiley and Sons, New York

Bongaarts, J.A. (1978) 'Framework for analysing proximate determinants of fertility'. *Population and Development Review*, 4: 105–32

Bowler, D.P. (1968) 'Prospects for family planning'. Paper Presented to First Seminar on the Demography of Papua New Guinea. The Australian National University

Brass, W. (1975) *Methods for Estimating Fertility and Mortality from Limited and Defective Data*. Laboratories for Population Statistics, Carolina Population Center, Chapel Hill

———— *et al.* (1968) *The Demography of Tropical Africa*. Princeton University Press, Princeton

Bulmer, R.N.H. (1971) 'Traditional forms of family limitation in New Guinea'. In M.W. Ward *et al.* (eds.), *Population Growth and Socio-Economic Change, New Guinea Research Bulletin No. 42*, pp. 137–62

Bumpass, L.L. (1973) 'Is low fertility here to stay?' *Family Planning Perspectives*, 5: 67–9

Caldwell, J.C. & Caldwell, P. (1977) 'The role of marital sexual abstinence in determining fertility'. *Population Studies*, 31(2): 193

Callan, V.J. & Wilks, J. (1982) 'Family size intentions and attitudes to contraception: Australian and Papua New Guinean youth'. *Australian Journal of Sex, Marriage and Family*, 3: 89–94

Cantrelle, P. & Leridon, H. (1971) 'Breast-feeding, mortality in childhood and fertility in a rural zone of Senegal'. *Population Studies*, 25(3)

Chinnery, E.W.P. (1926) 'Vital statistics with regard to the natives of the mandated territory of New Guinea'. International Health Congress

———— (1931) 'Studies of the Native Population of the East Coast of New Ireland'. *Territory of New Guinea Anthropological Report 6*

—— (1932–3) 'Census and population'. *Oceania*, 3(2): 214–17

Cho, L.-J. *et al.* (1970) *Differential Current Fertility in the United States*. University of Chicago Press, Chicago

Christie, J. & Radford, A.J. (1972) 'A report of a village family planning unit'. *Papua New Guinea Medical Journal*, 15(3): 165–7

Cilento, R.W. (1923) 'The depopulation of the Pacific'. *Second Pan-Pacific Science Congress*, Australia, Proceedings 2: 1395–9

—— (1924) 'Causes of depopulation among some island people'. *Medical Journal of Australia*, 2: 486

—— (1928) *The Causes of the Depopulation of the Western Islands of the Territory of New Guinea*. Government Printer, Canberra

Coale, A.J. (1978) 'Population growth and economic development: The case of Mexico'. *Foreign Affairs*, 56 (January): 415–29

Coale, A.J. & Demeny, P. (1967) *Regional Model Life Tables and Stable Populations*. Princeton University Press, Princeton

—— (1967) In Manual IV, *Methods of Estimating Basic Demographic Measures from Incomplete Data*. United Nations, New York

Coale, A.J. & Hoover, E.M. (1958) *Population Growth and Economic Development in Low-Income Countries*. Princeton University Press, Princeton

Cowgill, D.O. (1963) 'Transition theory as general population theory'. *Social Forces*, 41 (March): 270–4

Davis, K. & Blake, J. (1956) 'Social structure and fertility: An analytical framework'. *Economic Development and Cultural Change*, 4: 211–35

Davis, K. (1963) 'The theory of change and response in modern demographic history'. *Population Index* 29 (October): 345–66

—— (1967) 'Population policy: Will current programs succeed?'. *Science* (November) 730–9

—— (1973) 'Zero Population Growth: The Goal and the Means'. *Daedalus (Fall)*: 15–30

Dempwolff, O. (1904) 'Uber aussterbende Volker die Eingeborenem der Westlichen Inselm' in Dutsch — Neu-Guinea

Dow, T.E. (1977) 'Breastfeeding and abstinence among the Yoruba'. *Studies in Family Planning*, 8(8): 208–14

Epstein, A.L. & Epstein, T.A. (1962) 'A note on population in two Tolai settlements'. *Journal of the Polynesian Society*, 71(1): 10–82

Fawcett, J.T. (1977) *The Value and Cost of Children: Converging Theory and Research*. East-West Population Institute, Honolulu

Feeney, G. (1976) 'Estimating infant mortality rates from child survivorship data by age of mother'. *Asian and Pacific Census Newsletter*, 3(2): 12–16

Frederiksen, H. (1968) 'Determinants and consequences of mortality trends in Ceylon', In D.M. Heer (ed.), *Readings on Population*. Prentice-Hall, Englewood Cliffs

Freedman, R., Tze-Hwa Fan, Sou-Pen Wei & Mary Beth Weinberger (1977) 'Trends in fertility and in the effects of education on fertility in Taiwan, 1961–1974'. *Studies in Family Planning*, 8: 11–18

Gregory, J.L. (1955) 'Lihir patrol of April and May 1954'. *Papua New Guinea Medical Journal*, 1(1): 27–8

Hastings, P. (1973) *New Guinea: Problems and Prospects*. Cheshire Publishing Pty, Ltd., Melbourne

Holland, E.A. (1931) *Depopulation, East Coast, Kavieng*. Official Report to the Director of Public Health, Territory of New Guinea

Jackson, J.H.S. (1924) 'Causes of depopulation among some island peoples'. *Medical Journal of Australia*, 1: 58–61

Jain, A.K. & Bongaarts, J. (1981) 'Breastfeeding: Patterns, Correlates, and Fertility Effects'. *Studies in Family Planning*, 12(2): 79–99

Knodel, J. & Debavalya, N. (1978) 'Thailand's reproductive revolution'. *International Family Planning Perspective and Digest*, 4 (Summer): 34–49

────── (1980) 'Breastfeeding in Thailand: Trends and differentials'. *Studies in Family Planning*, 11(12): 355–77

Kopp, K. (1913) 'The native population of New Britain. Do they decline? And what are the causes?' *Rabaul Gazette*, 2(1): 8–12

Malcolm, L.A. (1969) 'Child mortality and disease pattern: Recent changes in the Bundi area'. *Papua New Guinea Medical Journal*, 12(1): 13–17

────── (1970) 'Growth malnutrition and mortality in the infant and toddler of the Asai valley of the New Guinea highlands'. *American Journal of Clinical Nutrition*, 23(8): 1090–5

Mauldin, W.P. (1978) 'Patterns of fertility decline in developing countries, 1950–75'. *Studies in Family Planning*, 9 (April): 75–84

Mauldin, W.P. & Berelson, B. (1978) 'Conditions of fertility decline in developing countries, 1965–75'. *Studies in Family Planning*, 9(5): 84–147

McDevitt, T.M. (1979) 'Mortality trends, patterns and causes'. In R. Skeldon *et al.* (ed.), *The Demography of Papua New Guinea*. Monograph 11. Institute of Applied Social and Economic Research, Boroko

Morauta, L. (1982) *Families, Households and Housing in the Population of Papua New Guinea*. ESCAP/SPC Country Monograph Series, United Nations, New York

Muirden, N.M. (1976) 'Family-planning services in Papua New Guinea'. Paper presented to Twelfth Symposium of the Medical Society of Papua New Guinea

Murray, J.H.P. (1925) 'The population problem in Papua'. In Second Pan-Pacific Science Congress, 1923, 1: 231–40

Nag, M. (1962) *Factors Effecting Human Fertility in Non-Industrial Societies: A Cross-Cultural Study, No. 66*. Department of Anthropology, Yale University

Notestein, F.W. (1953) 'The economics of population and food supplies'. *Proceedings of the Eighth International Conference of Agricultural Economists*, London

Nou-Taboro, O. (1978) 'Childhood mortality and expectation of life in Papua New Guinea: Estimates based on the 1971 Census'. Unpublished B.A. honours thesis, University of Papua New Guinea

O'Collins, M. (1979) 'Family-planning programmes in Papua New Guinea and Solomon Islands'. Paper presented at the Australian and New Zealand Association for the Advancement of Science, 49th Congress, Auckland, New Zealand

Oechsli, F.W. & Kirk, D. (1975) 'Modernization and the demographic transition in Latin America and the Caribbean'. *Economic Development and Cultural Change*, 23(3): 391–419

Papua and New Guinea, Territory of, Bureau of Statistics (1966) *Population Census; Preliminary Bulletins 20–38*. Port Moresby

Papua New Guinea, Bureau of Statistics (1971) *Population Census; Population Characteristics Bulletins 1–27*. Port Moresby

Papua New Guinea, National Statistical Office (1980) *Population Census; Preliminary Report*. Port Moresby

Powdermaker, H. (1931) 'Vital statistics of New Ireland as revealed in genealogies'. *Human Biology* 3(3): 351–75

Rafiq, M. (1977) *Demographic surveys of Papua New Guinea: A report on selected areas of Central and Northern Provinces with emphasis on fertility*. Port Moresby: Government Printer

────── (n.d.) *Population Profile 15, Papua New Guinea*. United Nations Fund for Population Activities, New York

125

——— (1978) *Demographic Survey of Kainantu Area: A Report with Special Emphasis on Fertility*. Government Printer, Port Moresby

——— (1979) 'Measurements of changes and differentials in fertility'. In R. Skeldon *et al.* (eds.), *The Demography of Papua New Guinea*. Monograph 11. Institute of Applied Social and Economic Research, Boroko

——— (1979) 'Some evidence on recent demographic changes in Papua New Guinea'. *Population Studies*, 33(2): 307–12

Refshauge, J.J. (1950) *Depopulation Survey — East Coast Road, New Ireland*. Report to the Director of Public Health, Territory of Papua and New Guinea.

Ruzicka, L.T. & Kanitkar, T. (1973) 'Infant mortality in greater Bombay'. *Demography India*, 2(1): 41–55

Ryder, N.B. (1976) 'Some sociological suggestions concerning the reduction of fertility in developing countries'. *Papers of the East-West Population Institute*, No. 37 (January)

Scragg, R.F.R. (1957) *Depopulation in New Ireland. A Study of Demography and Fertility*. Department of Public Health Monograph 3

——— (1967) Mortality Decline in a Sample Population in New Guinea. In IUSSP Contributed Papers, Sydney, 21–5 (August)

——— (1968) 'Population change over 20 years in rural New Guinea communities'. Paper presented to 1st Seminar on the Demography of Papua New Guinea, Australian National University

Singarimbun, M. & Manning, C. (1976) 'Breastfeeding, amenorrhea and abstinence in a Javanese village: A case study of Mojalama'. *Studies in Family Planning*, 7(6)

Skeldon, R. (1977) 'Family planning in the Goroka area of the Eastern Highlands'. *Discussion Paper No. 10*, IASER, Boroko

——— (1979) *The Demography of Papua New Guinea*. Monograph 11. Institute of Applied Social and Economic Research, Boroko

——— (1980) 'Recent urban growth in Papua New Guinea'. *Australian Geographer*, vol. 14, no. 5

Strathern, M. (1971) *Women in Between: Female Roles in a Male World: Mt. Hagen, New Guinea*. Seminar Press, New York

Sullivan, J.M. (1972) 'Models for the estimation of the probability of dying between birth and the exact ages of early childhood'. *Population Studies*, 26: 79–97

Teitelbaum, M.S. (1975) 'Relevance of demographic transition theory for developing countries'. *Science*, 188(4187): 420–5

Thompson, W.S. (1929) 'Plenty of people'. *American Journal of Sociology*, 34: 959–75

Trussell, J.T. (1975) 'A re-examination of the multiplying factors for the Brass technique for determining childhood survivorship rates'. *Population Studies*, 29: 97–107

United Nations (1956) 'Methods of appraisal of the quality of basic data for population estimates'. *Population Studies*, No. 23, Manual 11. United Nations, New York

——— (1963) *Population Bulletin No. 7: Conditions and Trends of Fertility in the World*. United Nations, New York

United Nations (1983) *Manual X Indirect Techniques for Demographic Estimation*. Department of International Economic and Social Affairs, New York

Van de Kaa, D.J. (1971) 'The demography of Papua New Guinea's indigenous population'. PhD thesis, Australian National University, Canberra

Vial, L.G. (1937/38) 'Some statistical aspects of population in the Morobe district, New Guinea'. *Oceania*, 8(4): 383–97

Watson, E.J. (1973) 'An experience of 2000 woman months of Lippes loop in the Highlands'. *Papua New Guinea Medical Journal*, 16(3): 145–8

Watson, W.B. (1975) *Family Planning in the Developing World*. The Population Council, New York

Williams, F.E. (1932/33) 'Depopulation and administration'. *Oceania*, 3(2): 218–26

World Bank (1984) *World Development Report 1984*. Oxford University Press, Oxford

——— (1972) *Population Planning: Sector Working Paper*. World Bank, Washington, D.C.

Appendix A

Male and Female Questionnaire
English Version

A STUDY OF FERTILITY, MORTALITY AND CONTRACEPTIVE USE IN PAPUA NEW GUINEA

A PROJECT OF THE DEMOGRAPHY UNIT
GEOGRAPHY DEPARTMENT
UNIVERSITY OF PAPUA NEW GUINEA
P.O. BOX 4820, UNIVERSITY

SPONSORING ORGANIZATIONS
1. 'Population Research Programme' of Papua New Guinea in co-operation with the Office of Environment and Conservation.
2. University of Papua New Guinea

PRINCIPAL INVESTIGATOR
Dr William K.A. Agyei

RESEARCH ASSOCIATES
Dr Reia Taufa
Dr Rafael Esmundo

DATE

NUMBER OF QUESTIONNAIRE

TOWN/VILLAGE

PROVINCE

DISTRICT

HOUSE SECT. LOT/NO. IN VILLAGE

INTERVIEWER'S NAME

SUPERVISOR'S NAME

LANGUAGE USED

INTERRUPTIONS

OTHERS PRESENT

CODER'S NAME

<u>MALE QUESTIONNAIRE</u>

Interviewer: Introduce yourself and explain about the interview.

I should like to begin by asking you some questions about the people who usually live here with you, in this household.

1.   How many people live in this household?

   ☐

Could you tell me the names of all the people who live here, including those who are away temporarily? I do not want to know about anyone who has been away more than six months.

Interviewer: List all persons, except the respondent, on the household membership chart, starting with the respondent's wife and their children, followed by other members of the household.

If the respondent is not married, start with the head of the household, then his/her spouse and their children followed by other members of the household.

The head of the household is the person to whom the house belongs (in the village), or who is responsible for paying the rent and rates (in a town).

Include all persons who normally live in the household, but not anyone who has been away for more than six months.

Ask each question on the household membership chart, for one member of the household at a time. If a person's age is not known, find out if the year is known.

HOUSEHOLD MEMBERSHIP CHART

2	3	4	5	6	7	8	9	10	11	12
Please give me the names of the persons who usually live in your household.	What is the relationship of this person to you?	Is this person male or female	How old is this person? If age not known ask year of birth Age Y.O.B.	Has this person been to school? Yes No Community Secondary Tertiary Mission	Is this person married divorced single separated widowed?	Does he/she work for wages Yes No	What does he/she earn per week?	In which province was he/she born?	Does he/she belong to a church? Yes No What church is that?	Did he/she sleep here last night?

When this is finished you must check.

I will read out the names of all the persons living here. Is there anyone else?

Yes   No

If there has been an omission, correct the number and add the personal details to the chart.

You now have to get the same information from the respondent.

13.   How old are you?

If the respondent does not know his age.

13a.   In what year were you born?

If the respondent does not know this you must enter an estimate of his age. How old do you think this person is?

14.   In what province were you born?

15.   Do you belong to a church?

Yes   No

15a.   Which church do you belong to?

16.   Have you ever attended school?

Yes   No

16a.   What was the highest level
       of education you reached?

Primary Grade

Secondary Grade

Technical College

Teachers' College

University

Other Tertiary - - - - -

Other - - - - - - - - - -   Please state.

17.   Do you have a source of income from
      any of the following?

(a)   a regular wage job

(b)   your own business

(c)   casual or part-time work

(d)   handicrafts

(e)   vegetable and fruit sales

(f)   betelnut sales

(g)   Pig farming

                                    Please state.
(h)   other - - - - - - - - - - - -

If respondent answers yes for a, b or c, ask Q.17a.

17a.   What sort of work do you do?

136

*If respondent answers yes for any source
of income, ask Q.17b.*

17b.   How much money do you earn?

      (a)   weekly

      (b)   fortnightly

      (c)   monthly

      (d)   yearly

18.   Are you married   divorced   widowed   separated   single

18a.   How many wives do you have?

18b.   How long did your marriage last?

Skip to Q.23

If respondent has only one wife skip to question 21.

If respondent has more than one wife ask questions 19 and 20.

19.   How long have you been married to each of your wives?

    first   second   third   fourth   fifth   sixth

20.   Have any of your marriages ended
      in death or divorce?

      Yes ☐   No ☐

      20a.   How many?

             Divorce ☐
             Death   ☐   *Skip to Q.22.*

Interviewer: *If respondent has been married twice,*
                 ask how 1st marriage ended.

                 If respondent has been married 3
                 times, ask how 1st and 2nd marriage
                 ended.

                 If respondent has been married 4
                 times, ask how 1st, 2nd and 3rd
                 marriage ended?

21.   How many times have you been married?

      Once   twice   three times   four times   or   more
      ☐   ☐   ☐   ☐   ☐

             How did your first marriage end?

                 death   divorce
                 ☐   ☐

             How did your second marriage end?

                 death   Divorce
                 ☐   ☐

How did your third marriage end?

death   divorce

□   □

22.   How old were you when you first got married?

[   ]

For this survey we want to know about all
the children that men and women have.
Could you please tell me about all your
children.

                                    Yes   No

23.   Do you have any children living?   □   □

23a.   How many sons do you have
        living?
□

23b.   How many daughters do you have
        living?
□

24. Have any children of yours died?   Yes ☐   No ☐

24a. How many sons have died?
☐

24b. How many daughters have died?
☐

25. Have any of your children been dead at birth?   Yes ☐   No ☐

25a. How many sons have been dead at birth?
☐

25b. How many daughters have been dead at birth?
☐

26. Have you adopted any children?   Yes ☐   No ☐

26a. How many sons have you adopted?
☐

26b. How many daughters have you adopted?
☐

140

27. Have any of your children been adopted?

Yes ☐ No ☐

27a. How many sons of yours have been adopted by others?
☐

27b. How many daughters of yours have been adopted by others?
☐

Do not ask question 28 and 29 of single men and men with no children.

28. Has your wife/wives had a baby in the last twelve months?

Yes ☐ No ☐

28a. Was that baby a boy or a girl?

Boy ☐
Girl ☐

29. Would you like more, less or the same number of children as you already have?

more	less	same	Don't know	God decides	Beyond my control
☐	☐	☐	☐	☐	☐

29a. How many more/less sons would you like to have?

number ☐   don't know ☐

29b.   How many more/less daughters
       would you like to have?

number   don't know
☐   ☐

Do not ask question 30 of single men.

30.   Is your wife/wives pregnant now?   Yes   No
                                           ☐   ☐

30a.   Would you prefer a boy or a
       girl?

                    Girl   ☐
                    Boy   ☐
                    Doesn't matter ☐
                    Don't know   ☐

31.   Do you believe in breast feeding?   Yes   No
                                           ☐   ☐

31a.   Why do you believe in breast
       feeding?

       ┌─────────────────────────────────┐
       └─────────────────────────────────┘

31b.   Why do you not believe in
       breast feeding?

       ┌─────────────────────────────────┐
       ├─────────────────────────────────┤
       └─────────────────────────────────┘

Do not ask question 32 of men with no children.

32. Have all your children been breastfed?

Yes   No
☐   ☐

32a. Why were some of your children
not breastfed?

I want to ask some questions now about the
way men and women plan to have their children, and whether they can prevent or delay
pregnancies.

33. How old do you think a woman's youngest
child should be before the next child
is born?

One year	
Two years	
Three years	
Four years	
Don't know	
Other	

33a. How would you and your wife
prevent having a baby before
_____ years?

34.   Should a man and wife go without
      sexual relations after a child
      is born?

Yes   No

34a. How long should this time be?

Interviewer: *Describe each method separately then after each desc-*
                 ription ask questions 35.

                 If the respondent answers yes to question 35, ask
                 question 36, then questions 37 and 39 if appropriate
                 before going on to the next method.

Descriptions of Method:

Some women get medicine from other women in the village to
prevent having children.

Some women breastfeed their babies in order to prevent
having children.

Some women take a pill every day to prevent having children.

Some women have an injection every 3 months to prevent
having children.

Some women have a loop placed in their wombs by a doctor
to prevent having children.

Some men use a condom to prevent their wives having children.

Some couples avoid sex on certain days to prevent having
children.

Some men practise withdrawal, that is, they are careful to
pull out before climax, to prevent their wives having
children.

Some men and women go without sex for several months or
longer to prevent having children.

Interviewer: Ask these questions after each method is described.

	35 Have you ever heard of this method? Yes / No	36 Have you and your wife used this method? Yes / No	37 Are you and your wife us-ing this method now? Yes / No	38 Why did you stop using this method? Record answer	39 After which birth did you and your wife use this method?
Village medicine					
Breastfeeding					
Pill					
Injection					
Loop					
Condom					
Ovulation					
Withdrawal					
Abstinence					

40.   Do you know of any other method of contraception?   Yes ☐   No ☐

40a.   What method is that?

40b.   Have you and your wife used this method?   Yes ☐   No ☐

Do not ask this question of single men.

Yes   No

41. Has your wife/wives ever become pregnant while you and your wife/wives were using a method of contraception?

    41a. What method of contraception were you and your wife using when she became pregnant?

42. Where did you learn these methods?

    Radio

    Newspaper

    Church

    Friends

    Clinic/Hospital

    Relatives

    Other   State other.

Yes   No

43. Can you discuss contraception with your wife?   *skip to Q.44*

Yes   No

    43a. Have you discussed contraception with your wife?

    43b. Why haven't you discussed contraception with your wife?

146

44. Why can't you discuss contraception
    with your wife?

    _____

45. Are contraceptives easily obtain-   Yes   No
    able at your clinic/hospital/aid   ☐   ☐
    post?

46. Are you and your wife/wives now   Yes   No
    using a form of contraception?   ☐   ☐

    46a. What method are you using
          now?

          _____

    46b. Why are you not using a
          method of contraception?

          _____

    46c. If you wished to use contra-   Yes   No
          ceptives do you know where   ☐   ☐
          to get them?

    46d. Where would you get contra-
          ceptives?

          _____

    46e. Would you use contraceptives   Yes   No
          if you know where to get   ☐   ☐
          them?

47. If a husband and wife are going to learn about contraceptives who should go and get the information?

Wife ☐

Husband ☐

Both ☐

Don't know ☐

48. Is there any person (other than your wife) who has any say in how many children you have?

Yes ☐   No ☐

48a. Who is that?

Men and women can have a special operation in hospital, called sterilization, that stops them having children.

49. Would you consider being sterilized when you have all the children that you want?

Yes ☐   No ☐

49a. Why would you not want to be sterilized?

Now there are some questions about your
children and the way you see other people's
children.

Do not ask questions 50 and 51 of men with no children.

	Yes	No
50. Are any of your children in school?	☐	☐

50a. How many of your children
are in school?

Boys ☐

Girls ☐

50b. How much money do you spend
in a year, on each child's
fees?

On your	K1-49	K50-99	K100-149	K150-199	K200-249	K250-299	K300+
1st child							
2nd child							
3rd child							
4th child							
5th child							
etc.							

	Yes	No
51. Do you have any school age children who are not in school?	☐	☐

51a. How many of your children
are not in school?

Boys ☐

Girls ☐

51b. Why are some of your children
not in school?

149

52. Who is it more important to send
     to school?

     A daughter

     A son

     Doesn't matter

     Don't know

                                           Yes   No
53. Do you expect your children to
     help you with money when you
     are old?

Do not ask this question of men with no children.

54. Would you say that your present family
     is big or small?

     Big

     Small

55. How many children make up a big
     family?

56. How many children make up a small
     family?

57. How many children should a village
     family have?

58. How many children should a town
     family have?

150

59.	What are the good things to be gained from a large family?

60.	What are the bad things about a large family?

61.	What are the good things to be gained from a small family?

62.	What are the bad things about a small family?

63.   Would you prefer to have more daughters or more sons?

Sons	Daughters	Doesn't matter	Don't know	God decides	Beyond my control
☐	☐	☐	☐	☐	☐

63a.   Why do you prefer more daughters/sons?

64.   Has your wife (wives) had a baby within the last twelve months that is now dead?

Yes ☐   No ☐

64a.   How old was that baby when it died?

64b.   Was the baby a boy or a girl?

Boy ☐

Girl ☐

65.   Has any other child of yours died   Yes   No
      in the last twelve months?   ☐   ☐

65a. How old was that child when
      it died?

      ☐

65b. Was that child a boy or a
      girl?

            Boy   ☐
            Girl ☐

66.   Has there been a death in your   Yes   No
      household, other than babies and   ☐   ☐
      children, in the last twelve
      months?

66a. Was that person male or
      female?

            Male   ☐
            Female ☐

66b. How old was that person when
      she/he died?

      ☐

66c. What was the cause of death?

      ☐

153

*If the dead person was female and in the age group 15-49 ask
Question 66d*

66d. When that woman died was she
pregnant or giving birth to
a child?

Pregnant

Childbirth   *tick appropriate
box*

No

If respondent answers 'no' to question 66d ask question 66e.

Yes   No

66e. When that woman died had she
recently given birth to a
baby?

66f. How old was the baby when she
died?

Interviewer: Check that you have asked all the questions.

Thank the respondent for his time and attention.

A STUDY OF FERTILITY, MORTALITY AND CONTRACEPTIVE USE IN PAPUA NEW GUINEA

A PROJECT OF THE DEMOGRAPHY UNIT
GEOGRAPHY DEPARTMENT
UNIVERSITY OF PAPUA NEW GUINEA
P.O. BOX 4820, UNIVERSITY

SPONSORING ORGANISATIONS
1. 'Population Research Programme' of Papua New Guinea in co-operation with the Office of Environment and Conservation.
2. University of Papua New Guinea

PRINCIPAL INVESTIGATOR
   Dr William K.A. Agyei

RESEARCH ASSOCIATES
   Dr Reia Taufa
   Dr Rafael Esmundo

DATE

NUMBER OF QUESTIONNAIRE

TOWN/VILLAGE

PROVINCE

DISTRICT

HOUSE SECT. LOT/NO. IN VILLAGE

INTERVIEWER'S NAME

SUPERVISOR'S NAME

LANGUAGE USED

INTERRUPTIONS

OTHERS PRESENT

CODER'S NAME

FEMALE QUESTIONNAIRE

Interviewer: *Introduce yourself and explain about the interview.*

I should like to begin by asking you some questions about the people who usually live here with you, in this household.

1.   How many people live in this household?

☐

Could you tell me the names of all the people who live here, including those who are away temporarily? I do not want to know about anyone who has been away more than six months.

Interviewer: *List all persons, except the respondent, on the household membership chart, starting with the respondent's husband and their children, followed by other members of the household.*

If the respondent is not married, start with the head of the household, then his/her spouse and their children followed by other members of the household.

The head of the household is the person to whom the house belongs (in the village), or who is responsible for paying the rent and rates (in a town).

Include all persons who normally live in the household, but not anyone who has been away for more than six months.

Ask each question on the household membership chart, for one member of the household at a time. If a person's age is not known, find out if the year of birth is known.

HOUSEHOLD MEMBERSHIP CHART

2	3	4	5	6	7	8	9	10	11	12
Please give me the names of the persons who usually live in your household.	What is the relationship of this person to you?	Is this person male or female?	How old is this person? If age not known ask year of birth Age Y.O.B.	Has this person been to school? Yes No Community Secondary Tertiary Mission	Is this person married divorced single separated widowed?	Does he/she work for wages? Yes NO	What does he/she earn per week?	In which province was he/she born?	Does he/she belong to a church? Yes No What church is that?	Did he/she sleep here last night?

When this is finished you must check.

I will read out the names of all the persons
living here. Is there anyone else?

Yes ☐ No ☐

*If there has been an omission, correct the number
and add the personal details to the chart.*

*You now have to get the same information from the
respondent.*

13.   How old are you?

☐

If the respondent does not know her age.

13a. In what year were you born?

☐

*If the respondent does not know this you must
enter an estimate of her age. How old do
you think this person is?*

☐

14.   In what province were you born?

☐

15.   Do you belong to a church?

Yes ☐ No ☐

15a.   Which church do you belong to?

☐

16.   Have you ever attended school?

Yes   No

☐   ☐

16a.   What was the highest level of
education you reached?

Primary Grade ☐
Secondary Grade ☐
Technical College ☐
Teachers' College ☐
University ☐
Other Tertiary_____ ☐
Other _ _ _ _ _ _ _ _ _ _   Please state.

17.   Do you have a source of income from
any of the following?

(a)   A regular wage job ☐
(b)   Your own business ☐
(c)   Casual or Part-Time Work ☐
(d)   Handicrafts ☐
(e)   Cash Crops ☐
(f)   Vegetable and Fruit Sales ☐
(g)   Betelnut Sales ☐
(h)   Pig Farming ☐
(i)   Other _ _ _ _ _ _ _ _ _ _ _ _ _ _ _ ☐   Please state.

If respondent answers yes for a, b or c, ask 17a.

17a.   What sort of work do you do?

☐

*If respondent answers yes for any
source of income ask 17b.*

17b.   How much money do you earn?

Weekly ☐
Fortnightly ☐
Monthly ☐
Yearly ☐

18.   Are you married, divorced, widowed, separated, single?

☐   ☐   ☐   ☐   ☐

18a.   How long have
        you been
        married to
        your present
        husband?

        ☐

                18b.   How long did your
                        marriage last?

                        ☐

                                        Interviewer: *Skip
                                                     to
                                                     Q.21*

Interviewer: *If respondent has been married twice, ask how 1st
                marriage ended.*

                *If respondent has been married 3 times, ask how
                1st and 2nd marriages ended.*

                *If respondent has been married 4 times, ask how
                1st, 2nd and 3rd marriages ended.*

19.   How many times have you been married?

Once   Twice   Three times   Four times   or   More
☐   ☐   ☐   ☐   ☐
Skip to
Q.20

                How did your first marriage end?

                        death   divorce
                        ☐   ☐

                How did your second marriage end?

                        death   divorce
                        ☐   ☐

                How did your third marriage end?

                        death   divorce
                        ☐   ☐

20.   How old were you when you first got
      married?

For this survey we want to know about all the
children each woman has had in her life. I
would like to ask you some questions about
your children.

                                                      Yes   No
21.   Do you have any children living?   ☐   ☐

      21a.   How many sons do you have living?
      ☐

      21b.   How many daughters do you have
             living?
      ☐

                                                      Yes   No
22.   Have any children of yours died?   ☐   ☐

      22a.   How many sons have died?
      ☐

      22b.   How many daughters have died?
      ☐

                                                      Yes   No
23.   Have you ever had a child that was dead   ☐   ☐
      at birth?

      23a.   How many of your sons have been
      ☐   dead at birth?

      23b.   How many of your daughters have
      ☐   been dead at birth?

24. Have you adopted any children?

Yes ☐ No ☐

24a. How many sons have you adopted?
☐

24b. How many daughters have you adopted?
☐

25. Have any of your children been adopted?

Yes ☐ No ☐

25a. How many sons of yours have
been adopted by others?
☐

25b. How many daughters of yours
have been adopted by others?
☐

26. Did you carry all your pregnancies to
full term?

Yes ☐ No ☐

26a. How long had you been pregnant
when it terminated?

26b. How did it terminate?

If the respondent has never given birth to a child living or dead, skip to question 40.

If the respondent has ever given birth to a child living or dead, fill out the pregnancy record form.

PREGNANCY RECORD FORM

Preg. Order	27 What name did you give your child?	28 How old were you then?	29 Did you have a boy or girl?	30 When was this child born?	31 Where was this child born? Village clinic hosp. aid post	32 Did you visit the clinic hosp. aid post regularly while pregnant?	33 Did you bring the child regularly to the cliinc after the birth?	34 Did you breast-feed this child?	35 How long did you breast-feed this child?	36 Did this child receive immuni-zation regularly?	37 Is this child still living?	38 How old was this child when it died?
			M F	Age M Y.O.B.				Yes No		Yes No	Yes No	

39. Would you like more, less or the same number of children as you already have?

			Don't	God	Beyond my
More	Less	Same	know	Decides	control
☐	☐	☐	☐	☐	☐

39a. How many more/less sons would you like to have?

Number   Don't know
☐   ☐

39b. How many more/less daughters would you like to have?

Number   Don't know
☐   ☐

40. Are you pregnant now?

Yes   No
☐   ☐

40a. Would you prefer a boy or a girl?

Girl	
Boy	
Don't care	
Don't know	

165

I want to ask some questions now, about the way men and women plan to have their children and whether they can prevent or delay pregnancies.

41. How old do you think a woman's youngest child should be before the next child is born?

1 year	
2 years	
3 years	
4 years	
don't know	
other	

41a. How would you and your husband prevent having a baby before _____ years?

42. Should a man and his wife go without sexual relations after a child is born?

Yes   No

42a. How long should this time be?

Interviewer : Do not ask this question of a woman with no children

43. Have you ever been pregnant and at the same time breastfeeding another child?

Yes   No

Interviewer: *Describe each method separately then after each description ask question 44.*

If the respondent answers yes to question 44, ask question 45, if the respondent answers no, go to the next method.

If the respondent answers yes to question 45, ask question 46, then questions 47 and 48 if appropriate before going on to the next method.

Description of Method:

Some women get medicine from other women in the village to prevent having children.

Some women breastfeed their babies in order to prevent having children

Some women take a pill every day to prevent having children.

Some women have an injection every 3 months to prevent having children.

Some women have a loop inserted into their wombs by a doctor to prevent having children.

Some men use a condom during sex to prevent their wives having children.

Some couples avoid sex on certain days to prevent having children.

Some men practise withdrawal, that is, they are careful and pull out before climax to prevent their wives having children.

Some men and women go without sex for several months longer to prevent having children.

	44 Have you ever heard of this method? Yes No	45 Have you ever used this method? Yes No	46 Are you curren-tly using this method Yes No	47 Why did you stop using this method? Record answer	48 After which birth did you use this method?
Village medicine					
Breast-feeding					
Pill					
Injection					
Loop					
Condom					
Ovulation					
Withdrawal					
Abstention					

49.　Do you know of any other method of contraception?　　Yes ☐　　No ☐

　　49a.　What method is that?

　　49b.　Have you ever used this method?　　Yes ☐　　No ☐

50. Have you ever become pregnant while you and your husband were using a method of contraception?

Yes □ No □

50a. What method of contraception were you using when you became pregnant?

51. Where did you learn of these methods?

Radio

Newspaper

Church

Friends

Clinic/Hospital

Relatives

Other _ _ _ _ _ _ _ _ _

State other.

Do not ask questions 52 and 53 of single women.

52. Can you discuss contraception with your husband?

Yes □ No □ *Skip to Q.53.*

52a. Have you discussed contraception with your husband?

Yes □ No □

52b. Why haven't you discussed contraception with your husband?

Skip to Q.54

169

53. Why can't you discuss contraception with your husband?

| |
| |

54. Are contraceptives easily obtainable at your clinic/hospital/aid post?

Yes ☐   No ☐

55. Are you (and your husband) using a form of contraception now?

Yes ☐   No ☐

55a. What method are you using now?

| |

Skip to Q.56

55b. Why are you not using a method of contraception?

| |
| |

55c. If you wished to use contraceptives do you know where to get them?

Yes ☐   No ☐

55d. Where would you get contraceptives?

| |

Skip to Q.56

55e. Would you use contraceptives if you knew where to get them

Yes ☐   No ☐

56.   If a husband and wife are going
      to learn about contraceptives who
      should go and get the information?

      Wife

      Husband

      Both

      Don't know

                                                    Yes   No

57.   Is there any person/s (other
      than your husband) who has any
      say in how many children you
      have?

          57a.   Who?

Men and women can have a special
operation, in hospital, called sterilization, that stops them having
children.

                                                    Yes   No

58.   Would you consider being steri-
      lized when you have all the
      children that you want?

          58a.   Why would you not want to
                 be sterilized?

Now there are some questions about your
children and the way you see other people's
children.

Do not aks questions 59 and 60 of women with no children.

59. Are any of your children in school?

Yes ☐   No ☐

    59a. How many of your children are in school?

Boys ☐
Girls ☐

    59b. How much money do you spend in a year on each child's school fees?

On your	K1–49	K50–99	K100–149	K150–199	K200–249	K250–299	K300+
1st child							
2nd child							
3rd child							
4th child							
5th child							
etc.							

60. Do you have any school age children who are not in school?

Yes ☐   No ☐

    60a. How many of your children are not in school?

Boys ☐
Girls ☐

    60b. Why are some of your children not in school?

61.   Who is it more important to send
      to school?

            A daughter

            A son

            Doesn't matter

            Don't know

                                              Yes   No

62.   Do you expect your children to
      help you with money when you are
      old?

            Do not ask question 63 of women with no
            children.

63.   **Would you say that your present**
      family is big or small?

                  Big

                  Small

64.   How many children make up a big
      family?

65.   How many children make up a small
      family?

66.   How many children should a village
      family have?

173

67. How many children should a town family have?

☐

68. What are the good things to be gained from a big family?

```
┌─────────────────────────────────────────────────────────┐
│                                                         │
├─────────────────────────────────────────────────────────┤
│                                                         │
├─────────────────────────────────────────────────────────┤
│                                                         │
└─────────────────────────────────────────────────────────┘
```

69. What are the bad things about a big family?

```
┌─────────────────────────────────────────────────────────┐
│                                                         │
├─────────────────────────────────────────────────────────┤
│                                                         │
├─────────────────────────────────────────────────────────┤
│                                                         │
└─────────────────────────────────────────────────────────┘
```

70. What are the good things to be gained from a small family?

```
┌─────────────────────────────────────────────────────────┐
│                                                         │
├─────────────────────────────────────────────────────────┤
│                                                         │
├─────────────────────────────────────────────────────────┤
│                                                         │
└─────────────────────────────────────────────────────────┘
```

71. What are the bad things about a small family?

```
┌─────────────────────────────────────────────────────────┐
│                                                         │
├─────────────────────────────────────────────────────────┤
│                                                         │
├─────────────────────────────────────────────────────────┤
│                                                         │
└─────────────────────────────────────────────────────────┘
```

72. Would you prefer to have more daughters or more sons?

Sons	Daughters	Doesn't matter	Don't know	God decides	Beyond my control
☐	☐	☐	☐	☐	☐

72a. Why do you prefer more daughters/sons?

```
┌─────────────────────────────────────────────────────────┐
│                                                         │
├─────────────────────────────────────────────────────────┤
│                                                         │
└─────────────────────────────────────────────────────────┘
```

Ask this question only of women with more than four children.

73. Suppose you could start having children from the beginning again. How many children would you have?

□

74. Have you had a baby within the last twelve months that is dead now?

Yes □   No □

74a. How old was the baby when it died?

[____]

74b. Was the child a boy or a girl?

Boy □
Girl □

75. Has any other child of yours died in the last twelve months?

Yes □   No □

75a. How old was the child when it died?

[____]

75b. Was the child a boy or a girl?

Boy □
Girl □

Yes   No

76. Has there been a death in your
     household, other than babies and
     children, in the last twelve
     months?

76a. Was that person a male or
      a female?

          male
          female

76b. What was the cause of death?

76c. How old was that person when
      she/he died?

*If the dead person was female and in the age group
15-49, ask question 76d.*

76d. When that woman died was she
      pregnant or giving birth to
      a child?

          pregnant   *Tick appropriate*
          childbirth   *box*
          no

If respondent answers no to question 76d ask question 76f.

                                                          Yes   No

76e.   When that woman died had
        she recently given birth
        to a baby?

76f.   How old was the baby when
        she died?

Interviewer: *Check that you have asked all the questions.*

                  Thank the respondent for her time and attention.

Appendix B

Interviewer's Manual

A STUDY OF FERTILITY, MORTALITY AND CONTRACEPTIVE
USE IN PAPUA NEW GUINEA

INTERVIEWER'S MANUAL

A PROJECT OF THE DEMOGRAPHY UNIT
GEOGRAPHY DEPARTMENT
UNIVERSITY OF PAPUA NEW GUINEA
P.O. BOX 4820, UNIVERSITY

SPONSORING ORGANISATIONS
1. 'Population Research Programme' of Papua New Guinea
   in co-operation with the Office of Environment and
   Conservation.
2. University of Papua New Guinea

PRINCIPAL INVESTIGATOR
  Dr William K.A. Agyei

RESEARCH ASSOCIATES
  Dr Reia Taufa
  Dr Rafael Esmundo

THE SURVEY AND ITS IMPORTANCE

The survey on which you will be working is a survey of fertility, mortality and contraception. More simply, it is about births, deaths and the way in which people plan to have children. The survey is being carried out by the Demography Unit of the University of Papua New Guinea in co-operation with the National Government Department of Health and the Office of Environment and Conservation. It also has the support of provincial governments. Information collected will be used by both the national and provincial governments for a number of different purposes, but the main reason for acquiring information about families is to facilitate a greater degree of efficiency in the planning of future government services.

In the past, societies in Papua New Guinea limited family size by traditional practices and health and environmental factors which reduced fertility or increased infant mortality. The advent of health services and socio-economic change in towns and villages has had the effect of breaking down traditional practices. As a result family size and infant survival rates have increased. The estimated annual growth rate of Papua New Guinea's population of 3 million people is approximately three per cent. This growth rate is already having an adverse effect on the availability of fertile land and will have long-term detrimental effects with regard to nutrition, education and employment opportunities.

The national government has a family-planning programme operating — to promote the use of contraception — in an attempt to confine Papua New Guinea's population within the limits of current resources. An important part of the survey is to gauge public opinion of this programme. This is achieved by asking rural and urban males and females about their views and practices with regard to an ideal family size, education and health services and contraceptive methods. In this respect, the recording of the respondent's age, educational standard and socio-economic status is of fundamental importance.

The improvement and expansion of family-planning services depends a great deal on the outcome of the survey. If the survey produces positive results then steps will be taken to create greater awareness of and accessibility to these services. This includes taking into account problems of communication and transport which inhibit continuity of supply to the establishments and which may deter people from taking advantage of what is available.

Awareness of fertility and mortality rates forms the basis of calculations of the population growth rate and allows for more constructive planning of provincial and national policies. By ascertaining the number of children in each family — the fertility levels of Papua New Guinean couples — and the majority opinion on ideal family size, the national and provincial governments are given guidelines in the policy planning and implementation of future educational, health and welfare services, housing schemes and transport requirements.

Knowledge of the mortality rate — the number of infants, children and adults who have died — also assists the governments in planning health services. A large number of deaths, particularly of infants and small children, indicates that either health services are not operating efficiently or the number of establishments is inadequate. A low death rate indicates the opposite — that health services are efficient and accessible.

Papua New Guinea does not have a population policy, that is, a national policy in which a rapid or slow increase in the population is encouraged. The interpretation of the information collected on this survey will provide a basis for the formulation of such a policy in accordance with the country's resources and changes in the life styles of the people. Because there is no law requiring people to register births and deaths, the Government is heavily dependent upon information of this nature collected by surveys like this and through the national census.

The success of this survey is therefore crucial for a number of reasons and depends very much on the skill and sensitivity of the interviewers. If the interviewers do not have the ability and patience to draw honest answers from their respondents, the survey will be inaccurate and worthless.

DETAILS OF THE SURVEY

1. The survey is being carried out in eight provinces in urban and rural areas and will involve about 8,000 people.
2. In each province approximately 500 people will be interviewed in an urban area and an equal number in a rural area.
3. Two-thirds of the people interviewed will be women in the age group 15–49, the childbearing age group. One-third of the people interviewed will be men in the age group 20–54.
4. In each household where *women* are interviewed *one woman in the age group 15–49 will be interviewed.*
5. In the households where *men* will be interviewed the head of the households will be interviewed. If the *head of the household* is not present *or* is a female, *one man in the age group 20–54 who lives in that house will be interviewed.*

THE ROLE OF THE INTERVIEWER

The role of the interviewer is very important for the success and accuracy of a survey like this one. It is up to the interviewer to ensure that the questions are understood and the right answers are given. The interviewer can only get honest answers from the person being interviewed if he/she has the full co-operation and confidence of the respondent. Interviewing well is not an easy task and there are a number of points you must know and understand before you start work as an interviewer. Here are some of the more important points to remember.

1. An interview involves two persons, one person, the interviewer, asks the questions and the other person, the respondent, provides the answers. Although this is different from the ordinary conversations you should try to keep the interview as friendly and informal as possible. Some questions will not be easy for the respondent to answer but a friendly attitude on your part will make it much easier for the person to answer.

2. Although you should be friendly and polite throughout the interview it is important that you do not allow your own opinions to be known to the respondent. Many people like to please other people and a respondent might try to impress you by giving the answers that he/she thinks will impress you rather than by giving the honest and correct answers. You must of course show interest in the answers you are given but never indicate your own feelings on any matter. If you are asked for an opinion explain as politely as possible that as an interviewer it is not your place to offer an opinion.

3. You must be very careful when asking questions that you do not change the meaning of a question. You should always ask a question exactly as it is written on the questionnaire. However, sometimes you will need to repeat or explain a question and this means that it is essential that you know what every question means. Remember that even a minor word change can alter the meaning of a question. If you have to reword a question or explain it you must know exactly what it means. If the meaning of a question is altered then the answer becomes meaningless for this survey. It is therefore most important that you understand every question perfectly before you begin interviewing.

4. You must listen very carefully to the answers that are given. It is no good asking questions if you are not willing to listen to the answers and record them accurately. You must always write down the answers immediately. If you do not do this you will forget what was said and will not record the correct answer. Remember, that if you do not write a correct answer the interview is worthless. It is a waste of the respondent's time. It is a waste of your time as well.

5. You need to be always on the lookout for mistakes in the respondent's answers. Some of the questions are very similar and you should be watching that the answers do not contradict each other, that is, that both answers cannot be true so one of them must be wrong. If you think that an answer is wrong, politely point out the error and blame yourself (I'm sorry I must have made a mistake) and ask the question again. You must always check back if you make a mistake.

6. It is always necessary to remain polite and friendly during the interview. In some cases you will be much younger than the person you are interviewing and the respondent may feel embarrassed talking to a younger person who may also be a stranger about such sensitive things as family-planning methods. Therefore, you must remain at all times aware of the respondent's feelings. It is important not to show embarrassment when asking a question as this is certain to cause embarrassment to the respondent. If you are embarrassed about asking

any questions in this survey you are not suitable to work as an interviewer because this could cause inaccurate answers to be given.

7. You must always be very patient and never rush an interview. Some of the people you will talk to will never have experienced an interview and it will be a very strange experience for them. It will take time for them to get used to you so you must never try to hurry an answer from a respondent. When you start losing patience it is time to stop interviewing.

In summary, the main points to remember are:

1. The interview should be as much like an everyday conversation as possible.
2. You must not let your own feelings and opinions influence the person you are interviewing.
3. You must ask the questions as they are written down. There may be occasions where a question will need to be explained and it is essential that you understand exactly what each question means.
4. You must listen carefully and record answers accurately and immediately.
5. You must constantly be on the look out for mistakes and contradictions.
6. You must remain polite, friendly and sympathetic throughout the interview. You must never show any embarrassment.
7. You must at all times be patient. Never rush an interview.

PROBLEMS WITH INTERVIEWING

Privacy

You must interview people by themselves if it is at all possible. This is because the respondent could change the answer to a question if another person is listening in order to give the answer that the other person will approve of rather than the one they really believe. Always make it clear that you wish to conduct the interview in private and if necessary ask if you can be alone with the respondent. If this fails ignore the other people.

Silence

Sometimes the respondent will remain silent instead of answering a question. This could be caused by a number of things: shyness, embarrassment, unwillingness to answer, the difficulty of the questions or simply not knowing the answer. If this happens first repeat the question as it is written. If the silence continues you must decide why the respondent is not answering.

If you think a respondent has not understood the question ask him or her

185

directly if he/she understands the question. If a respondent does not understand the question repeat it in a slightly different way, using simple words and taking care not to alter the meaning. It is in this sort of situation that it is very important that you understand what a question means.

If silence is caused by shyness or embarrassment, tell the respondent that there is no need to feel shy or embarrassed as the information is private and will not be made known to any other persons. Point out also that many other people are being asked the same question, but most important, sympathy and kindness is what is needed in this situation.

Don't know

'Don't Know' answers arise for much the same reasons as silences occur and once again you have to try to decide why you have not received an answer. If you think that embarrassment or shyness is the cause, reassure the respondent that the interview is private. If the respondent does not understand the question, reword it or explain what is wanted. If the respondent has difficulty in remembering try to help him or her to remember. For example, if a question like, 'For how long did you breastfeed?' gets a 'don't know' answer, try to assist by asking, 'Was it a short or long time?' or, 'When was the baby weaned?'

Time and age

Often people will have trouble with questions about time and age. With children it is probably a good idea to ask if a clinic book is available. If not, the provided list of 'notable events' can be used to help you estimate the ages of people who do not know or are not sure of their ages or the ages of other household members. The use of 'notable events' will be discussed in detail during training.

Incorrect answers

As has been said earlier, an interviewer must always be on the watch for incorrect answers. When you think that you have discovered a mistake, politely mention it, blame yourself and ask the question again. You must always check if you suspect that a mistake has been made.

Incorrect recording of answers

You must always record the answer to each question straight away. If you leave an answer, you will not remember it later. Remember, every question has an answer and every answer must be recorded even if it is a 'don't know' or a refusal to answer.

INSTRUCTIONS

There are a number of instructions on the questionnaire that you must understand if you are going to complete it correctly:

Italics

All parts of the interview printed in italics are instructions to the interviewer and should not be read out.

Arrows

Many questions consist of more than one part. Questions that follow on from the main question are labelled a, b, c, etc. But often, not every part of each question is asked of all respondents. For example, question 21, on the female questionnare asks 'Do you have any children living?' and is followed by questions 21a and 21b, that ask about the sex of those children. Questions 21a and 21b are only asked of respondents who answer 'yes' to question 21. This is indicated by the use of arrows, e.g.

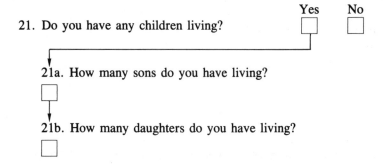

You must follow the arrows carefully. If a respondent gives an answer that is followed by an arrow you must follow the arrow. If there is no arrow you go on to the next question.

Skip instructions

Not every question has to be asked of each respondent and sometimes there will be an instruction to skip a certain question or questions. You must follow these instructions carefully or you could ask someone an irrelevant or embarrassing qustion and lose your chance of completing the interview.

Boxes

Some questions have simple 'yes' or 'no' answers, in this case you tick the appropriate box. Other questions have a number of possible answers and you should tick the box beside the answer the respondent gives. Often there is a box marked 'other'. This box is ticked when an answer other than those listed is given. In this case you not only tick the box provided but also write in the space provided what that answer was.

Other instructions

Sometimes, just before a question or questions there will be an instruction in italics instructing you not to ask that question or questions of certain persons. Again, to avoid embarrassing or irritating a respondent you must take care to follow such instructions.

Interviewers' Instructions — Male

Question No.	Instructions
1	You must find out the total number of people who usually live in that household. You should include persons who are temporarily absent but no one who has been absent for longer than six months. Please remember to include the respondent as well.

2–12   You must ask each question about every member of the household separately. Most of the questions are straightforward but there are some points you must remember to enable you to complete this section accurately.

Question 5 If neither the age nor the year of birth are known use notable events to try and estimate the age or, in the case of children, ask for clinic books. It will sometimes be difficult to get accurate ages as the persons will not always be present. You must just be patient and do your best.

Question 6 You must first find out if the person has had any formal education. If he or she has had none then write 'no' in column 6. If he or she has been to school find out the highest level of education reached and record that in column 6.

Question 9 Do not ask this question of people who do not work for wages.

Question 11 If a person belongs to a church write the name of the church in column 11. If he/she does not belong to a church write 'no' in column 11.

13   If a respondent does not know his age or year of birth use significant events to estimate the age.

14–15   These are straightforward questions about the respondent's province of birth and church membership.

16   If the respondent has ever attended school you must record the highest level of education the respondent has had.

On the questionnaire is listed a number of different levels of education the respondent may have had. You should write in the box beside the appropriate level the number of years completed at that level.

e.g. Primary Grade $\boxed{5}$

This means that the respondent completed up to grade five at primary school.

Secondary Grade $\boxed{10}$

This means that the respondent completed up to grade ten at secondary school.

University $\boxed{3}$

This means that the respondent completed three years at the university level.

There are two sections 'other tertiary' and 'other' which should be used when the type of schooling that the respondent has had is not listed.

'Other tertiary' means an educational institution attended after completion of at least grade ten. Examples of this would be fisheries and agricultural colleges, seminaries, health colleges and nursing schools.

'Other' includes any other form of eduation and could include 'Tok Ples' school, pidgin school and vocational school.

It is important that if the person was educated in an 'other tertiary' or 'other' educational institution that you record on the line provided what school that was.

e.g. other vocational $\boxed{1}$

Means that the respondent spent one year at vocational school.

17   Read out the options and tick the box opposite the source of income of the respondent. If the respondent has no source of income write 'none' beside question 17 and go to question 18. If the respondent had a source of income other than those listed tick the box opposite 'other' and record what the source of income is on the line provided.

If the respondent answers 'yes' to a, b or c ask question 17a. If the respondent has any source of income you must ask question 17b. If the respondent does not know his weekly income ask if he knows his fortnightly, monthly or yearly income. If the person does not know his income write 'don't know' beside question 17b.

18–21	This is a quite complicated section and it is most important that you take care to follow the instructions. This include arrows, skip instructions and instructions in italics.
22	This is a straightforward question about the age at which the respondent first got married. Do not ask this question of single men.
23–25	These are straightforward questions about the respondents' own children.
26	Make sure that the respondent understands that the children we want to know about here are the children born to someone else that he has adopted.
27	Make sure that the respondent understands that the children that we want to know about here are children born to his wife or wives who have been adopted by others.
28–30	These are straightforward questions not to be asked of men who are single.
31	This is a straightforward question but make sure that you follow the arrows.
32	This is a straightforward question not to be asked of men with no children.
33	If the answer is other than those items given by the respondent record in the box opposite 'other'. In question 33a insert the answer given in 33 on the dotted line.
34	This is a straightforward question.
35–39	This is probably the most difficult section of the questionnaire so you must be very careful when asking these questions that you do not upset anybody. There are instructions at the top of the page on the order in which you must ask the questions but a little common sense should tell you when not to ask a question. For example, if a respondent answers 'no' to question 35, that

is, the respondent has never heard of the method described, then it is obvious that they have not used the method and there is no point in asking any more questions about that method. You then ask question 35 for the next method and so on. Similarly, you do not ask any more questions if the respondent answers 'no' to question 36.

It is important that you study this particular section and know exactly what you have to do. This section is a real test of your ability as an interviewer.

40   This question is straightforward except that if the man is single you must leave out the words 'and your wife' if you need to ask question 40b and ask instead, 'Have you used this method?'

41   This is a straightforward question but do not ask this question of single men.

42   Tick the appropriate box. If the source of information is other than those given tick the 'other' box and write the source on the dotted line.

43   Make sure you follow the arrows and skip instructions. Do not ask this question of single men.

44   This is a straightforward question but do not ask this question of single men.

45   A straightforward question.

46   Make sure you follow the arrows as this is quite a complicated section. Leave out the words 'and your wife/wives' if the respondent is single. Ask instead, 'Are you now using any form of contraception?'

47   Tick the appropriate box.

48   This is a straightforward question but leave out the words 'other than your wife' if the respondent is single.

49   This is a straightforward question.

50–51   These are both straightforward questions but do not ask them of men with no children.

52	Tick the appropriate box.
53–58	These are straightforward questions.
59–62	Ask the respondent each question and record all the answers that he gives immediately. When he has finished ask again if there are any more comments on these questions. Record all the answers immediately. If you do not do this you will forget.
63	Tick the appropriate box. If the respondent has preference for either sons or daughters ask question 63a. If he prefers more daughters ask, 'Why do you prefer more daughters?' If he prefers more sons ask, 'Why do you prefer more sons?' This is a straightforward question but do not ask the question of single men. A baby is a child under the age of one year.
65	This is a straightforward question and includes any child of the respondent, even grown-up children, one year and older.
66	Follow the instructions carefully. Questions 66d, 66e and 66f are only asked if the person who died was a woman in the age group 15–49.

Interviewers' Instructions — Female

Question No.	Instructions
1	You must find out the total number of people who live in that household. You should include persons who are temporarily absent but no one who has been absent for longer than six months. Please remember to include the respondent as well.

2–12   You ask each question about every member of the household separately. Most of the questions are straightforward but there are some points you must remember to enable you to complete this section accurately.

Question 5 If neither the age nor the year of birth are known use notable events to try and estimate the age or, in the case of children, ask for clinic books. It will sometimes be difficult to get accurate ages as the persons will not always be present. You must just be patient and do your best.

Question 6 You must first find out if the person has had any formal education. If she has had none then record 'no' in column 6. If she has been to school find out the highest level of education reached and record that in column 6.

Question 9 Do not ask this question of people who do not work for wages.

Question 11 If a person belongs to a church write the name of the church in column 11. If she does not belong to a church write 'no' in column 11.

13   If a respondent does not know her age or year of birth use significant events to estimate the age.

14–15   These are straightforward questions about the respondent's province of birth and church membership.

16   If the respondent has ever attended school you must record the highest level of education she reached.

On the questionnaire is listed a number of different levels of education the respondent might have had. You should write in the box beside the appropriate standard the number of years completed at that level.

e.g. Primary Grade $\boxed{5}$

This means that the respondent completed up to grade five at primary school.

Secondary Grade $\boxed{10}$

This means that the respondent completed up to grade ten at secondary school.

University $\boxed{3}$

This means that the respondent completed three years at the university level.

There are two sections 'other tertiary' and 'other' which should be used when the type of schooling that the respondent has had is not listed.

'Other tertiary' means an educational institution attended after completion of at least grade 10. Examples of this would be fisheries and agricultural colleges, seminaries, health colleges and nursing schools.

'Other' includes any other form of eduation and could include 'Tok Ples' school, pidgin school and vocational school.

It is important that if the person was educated in an 'other tertiary' or 'other' educational institution that you record on the line provided what school that was.

e.g. other vocational $\boxed{1}$

This means that the respondent spent one year at vocational school.

17   Read out the options and tick the box opposite the source of income of the respondent. If the respondent has no source of income write 'none' beside question 17 and go to question 18. If the respondent has a source of income other than those listed tick the box opposite 'other' and record what the source of income is on the line provided.

If the respondent answers 'yes' to a, b or c ask question 17a. If the respondent has any source of income you must ask question 17b. If the respondent does not know his weekly income, ask if she knows her fortnightly, monthly or yearly income.

	If the person does not know her income write 'don't know' beside question 17b.
18	Tick the appropriate box then follow the arrows and skip instructions.
19	The instructions for question 19 are given before this question. Read them carefully.
20	This is a straightforward question about the age at which the respondent first got married. Do not ask this question of single women.
21–23	These are straightforward questions about the respondent's own children.
24	Make sure that the respondent understands that the children we want to know about here are children born to another woman that the respondent has adopted.
25	Make sure that the respondent understands that the children we want to know about here are children that she has given birth to that have been adopted by another person.
26	In this question we want to know about pregnancies that did not last the full nine months. That is, a woman becomes pregnant but only carries the baby for a few weeks or months.
27–28	You do not ask these questions of a woman who has never given birth to a child, living or dead. Ask each question for each child that the woman has given birth to, living or dead. Start with the first pregnancy, that is, the first-born child. Ask whether there are clinic books available for the children. These can be of considerable assistance with the details of a child.
39	You do not ask this question of women with no children.
40	This is a straightforward question.
41	If the answer is other than those items given write the answer given by the respondent in the box opposite 'other'. In question 41a insert the answer given in question 41 on the dotted line.

42   This is a straightforward question.

43   Do not ask this question of women with no children.

44–48   This is probably the most difficult section of the questionnaire
            so you must be very careful when asking these questions to
            make sure that you do not offend anyone.
            There are instructions at the top of the page on the order in
            which to ask questions 44–48 but a little common sense should
            tell you when not to ask a question. For example, if a respon-
            dent answers 'no' to question 44, that is, the respondent has
            never heard of the method described, then it is obvious that she
            will not have used the method so there is no point in asking
            more questions about this method. You then ask question 44
            of the next method and so on.
            Similarly, you do not ask anymore questions about a particular
            method if the respondent answers 'no' to question 45.
            It is important that you study this particular section and know
            exactly what you have to do. This section is a real test of your
            ability as an interviewer.

49   This is a straightforward question.

50   This is a straightforward question but if the respondent is
            single then you must leave out the words 'and your husband'.

51   Tick the appropriate box. If the source of the information is
            other than those given, tick the 'other' box and record the
            source on the dotted line.

52   Make sure you follow the arrows and skip instructions and do
            not ask this question of single women.

53   This is a straightforward question but do not ask this question
            of single women.

54   This is a straightforward question.

55   Make sure you follow the arrows and skip instructions
            carefully as this is quite a complicated section. Leave out the
            words 'and your husband' if the respondent is single. Ask
            instead, 'Are you now using a form of contraception?'

56   Tick the appropriate box.

57	This is a straightforward question but leave out the words 'and your husband' if the respondent is single.
58	This is a straightforward question.
59–60	These are both straightforward questions but they are not to be asked of women with no children.
61	Tick the appropriate box.
62	This is a straightforward question.
63	This is a straightforward question but do not ask this question of women with no children.
64–67	These are straightforward questions.
68–71	Ask the respondent each question and record all the answers she gives immediately. When she has finished, ask again if there are any more comments on these questions. Record all the answers immediately. If you do not do this you will forget.
72	Tick the appropriate box. If the respondent has a preference for either sons or daughters ask question 72a. If she prefers sons ask, 'Why do you prefer more sons?' If she prefers daughters ask, 'Why do you prefer more daughters?'
73	Straightforward but ask this question only of women with more than four children.
74	This is a straightforward question. A baby is a child less than one year of age.
75	This is a straightforward question and includes any child of the respondent, even grown-up children one year and older.
76	Follow the instructions carefully. Questions 76d, 76e and 76f are only asked if the person who died was a woman in the age group 15–49.

Appendix C1: Estimation of total fertility rate from the survey data for rural areas: Papua New Guinea

Age at time of survey (1)	Interval i (2)	Births per woman in 12 months preceding survey f_i (3)	Average number of children ever born P_i (4)	Cumulative fertility at beginning of interval $5\sum_{j=0}^{i-1} f_j$ (5)	Multiplying factors for estimating average value fertility w_i (6)	Estimated average cumulative fertility $F_i = 5\sum_{j=0}^{i-1} f_j + w_i f_i$ (7)	Adjusted age-specific fertility rates $(f_i' = f_i \times P_i/F_i)$		
							P_i/F_i (8)	P_2/F_2 (9)	P_3/F_3 (10)
15–19	1	0.105	0.154	0.000	1.568	0.165	0.933	0.108	0.108
20–24	2	0.286	1.351	0.525	2.763	1.315	1.027	0.294	0.295
25–29	3	0.298	2.929	1.955	2.971	2.840	1.031	0.306	0.307
30–34	4	0.229	4.241	3.445	3.086	4.152	1.021	0.235	0.236
35–39	5	0.173	5.102	4.550	3.200	5.104	0.999	0.178	0.178
40–44	6	0.098	5.609	5.415	3.411	5.749	0.976	0.101	0.101
45–49	7	0.061	6.484	5.905	4.009	6.150	1.054	0.063	0.063
Total		1.250						1.285	1.288
Total fertility rate		6.250						6.425	6.440

$f_1/f_2 = 0.267$; $\bar{m} = 30.3$

Appendix C2: Estimation of total fertility rate from the survey data for urban areas: Papua New Guinea

Age at time of survey (1)	Interval i (2)	Births per woman in 12 months preceding survey f_i (3)	Average number of children ever born P_i (4)	Cumulative fertility at beginning of interval $5 \sum_{j=0}^{i-1} f_j$ (5)	Multiplying factors for estimating average value fertility w_i (6)	Estimated average cumulative fertility $F_i = 5 \sum_{j=0}^{i-1} f_j + w_i f_i$ (7)	Adjusted age-specific fertility rates ($f_i' = f_i \times P_i/F_i$) P_i/F_i (8)	P_2/F_2 (9)	P_3/F_3 (10)
15–19	1	0.078	0.141	0.000	1.585	0.123	1.146	0.098	0.090
20–24	2	0.242	1.329	0.390	2.771	1.061	1.252	0.303	0.279
25–29	3	0.272	2.775	1.600	2.983	2.411	1.151	0.341	0.313
30–34	4	0.238	3.881	2.960	3.093	3.727	1.041	0.298	0.274
35–39	5	0.162	4.586	3.770	3.212	4.290	1.069	0.203	0.186
40–44	6	0.094	5.348	4.005	3.425	4.327	1.236	0.118	0.108
45–49	7	0.066	6.067	4.170	4.125	4.442	1.366	0.083	0.076
Total		1.152						1.444	1.326
Total fertility rate		5.760						7.220	6.630

$f_1/f_2 = 0.322$; $\bar{m} = 29.8$

Appendix C3: Estimation of total fertility rate from the survey data for borh rural and urban areas: Papua New Guinea

Age at time of survey (1)	Interval i (2)	Births per woman in 12 months preceding survey f_i (3)	Average number of children ever born P_i (4)	Cumulative fertility at beginning of interval $5\sum_{j=0}^{i-1} f_j$ (5)	Multiplying factors for estimating average value fertility w_i (6)	Estimated average cumulative fertility $F_i = 5\sum_{j=0}^{i-1} f_j + w_i f_i$ (7)	Adjusted age-specific fertility rates ($f'_i = f_i \times P_i/F_i$)		
							P_i/F_i (8)	P_2/F_2 (9)	P_3/F_3 (10)
15–19	1	0.087	0.145	0.000	1.568	0.136	1.066	0.101	0.098
20–24	2	0.258	1.338	0.435	2.763	1.148	1.165	0.300	0.291
25–29	3	0.283	2.891	1.725	2.971	2.566	1.127	0.330	0.319
30–34	4	0.233	4.123	3.140	3.086	3.859	1.068	0.271	0.263
35–39	5	0.168	4.933	4.305	3.200	4.843	1.019	0.196	0.189
40–44	6	0.097	5.554	5.145	3.411	5.476	1.014	0.113	0.109
45–49	7	0.063	6.338	5.560	4.009	5.813	1.090	0.073	0.071
Total		1.189						1.384	1.340
Total fertility rate		5.945						6.920	6.700

$f_1/f_2 = 0.337$; $\bar{m} = 30.2$

Appendix D1: Average number of children ever born (P_i), average number of deceased children and proportion dead (D_i) by current age and residence of mother: Papua New Guinea 1979–80

Age of mother	Interval (i)	Average number of children ever born (P_i)			Average number of deceased children			Proportion dead (D_i)		
		Males	Females	Both sexes	Males	Females	Both sexes	Males	Females	Both sexes
Rural areas										
15–19	1	0.079	0.075	0.154	0.009	0.008	0.017	0.114	0.107	0.110
20–24	2	0.692	0.659	1.351	0.084	0.074	0.158	0.121	0.112	0.117
25–29	3	1.494	1.435	2.929	0.214	0.198	0.412	0.143	0.138	0.141
30–34	4	2.176	2.065	4.241	0.357	0.316	0.673	0.164	0.153	0.159
35–39	5	2.618	2.484	5.102	0.483	0.445	0.928	0.184	0.179	0.182
40–44	6	2.867	2.742	5.609	0.604	0.557	1.161	0.211	0.203	0.207
45–49	7	3.319	3.165	6.484	0.810	0.718	1.528	0.244	0.227	0.236
Urban areas										
15–19	1	0.072	0.069	0.141	0.004	0.004	0.008	0.056	0.058	0.057
20–24	2	0.681	0.648	1.329	0.077	0.068	0.145	0.113	0.105	0.109
25–29	3	1.415	1.360	2.775	0.198	0.182	0.380	0.140	0.134	0.137
30–34	4	1.991	1.890	3.881	0.323	0.286	0.609	0.162	0.151	0.157
35–39	5	2.353	2.233	4.586	0.399	0.368	0.767	0.170	0.165	0.167
40–44	6	2.734	2.604	5.348	0.526	0.485	1.011	0.192	0.186	0.189
45–49	7	3.106	2.961	6.067	0.731	0.649	1.380	0.235	0.219	0.227
All sectors										
15–19	1	0.074	0.071	0.145	0.007	0.005	0.012	0.095	0.070	0.083
20–24	2	0.685	0.653	1.338	0.083	0.068	0.151	0.121	0.104	0.113
25–29	3	1.474	1.417	2.891	0.208	0.191	0.399	0.141	0.135	0.138
30–34	4	2.111	2.012	4.123	0.346	0.305	0.651	0.164	0.151	0.158
35–39	5	2.526	2.407	4.933	0.462	0.401	0.863	0.183	0.167	0.175
40–44	6	2.844	2.710	5.554	0.573	0.538	1.100	0.201	0.195	0.198
45–49	7	3.245	3.093	6.338	0.779	0.691	1.470	0.240	0.223	0.232

Appendix D2: Average number of children ever born (P_i), average number of deceased children and proportion dead (D_i) by region and current age of mother: Papua New Guinea 1979–80

Age of mother	Interval (i)	Average number of children ever born (P_i)			Average number of deceased children			Proportion dead (D_i)		
		Males	Females	Both sexes	Males	Females	Both sexes	Males	Females	Both sexes
Papua region										
15–19	1	0.076	0.072	0.148	0.007	0.005	0.012	0.092	0.069	0.081
20–24	2	0.675	0.644	0.319	0.078	0.070	0.148	0.116	0.109	0.112
25–29	3	1.436	1.380	2.816	0.200	0.185	0.385	0.139	0.134	0.137
30–34	4	2.100	1.993	4.093	0.341	0.644	0.162	0.162	0.152	0.157
35–39	5	2.518	2.390	4.908	0.439	0.406	0.845	0.174	0.170	0.172
40–44	6	2.877	2.732	5.609	0.553	0.513	1.066	0.192	0.188	0.190
45–49	7	3.214	3.063	6.277	0.761	0.675	1.436	0.238	0.220	0.229
Highlands region										
15–19	1	0.079	0.075	0.154	0.007	0.007	0.014	0.089	0.093	0.091
20–24	2	0.728	0.693	0.421	0.089	0.078	0.167	0.122	0.113	0.118
25–29	3	1.496	1.437	2.933	0.216	0.200	0.416	0.144	0.139	0.142
30–34	4	2.178	2.067	4.245	0.369	0.327	0.696	0.169	0.158	0.164
35–39	5	2.619	2.487	5.106	0.484	0.447	0.931	0.185	0.180	0.182
40–44	6	2.883	2.737	5.620	0.611	0.564	1.175	0.212	0.206	0.209
45–49	7	3.329	3.172	6.501	0.851	0.754	1.605	0.256	0.238	0.247
New Guinea Mainland region										
15–19	1	0.073	0.069	0.142	0.007	0.006	0.013	0.096	0.087	0.092
20–24	2	0.668	0.637	1.305	0.080	0.070	0.150	0.120	0.110	0.115
25–29	3	1.560	1.499	3.059	0.220	0.203	0.423	0.141	0.135	0.138
30–34	4	2.202	2.091	4.293	0.365	0.323	0.688	0.168	0.154	0.160
35–39	5	2.644	2.510	5.154	0.478	0.442	0.920	0.181	0.176	0.179
40–44	6	2.904	2.757	5.661	0.604	0.557	1.161	0.208	0.202	0.205
45–49	7	3.346	3.190	6.536	0.840	0.745	1.585	0.251	0.234	0.234
New Guinea Islands region										
15–19	1	0.075	0.071	0.146	0.006	0.005	0.011	0.080	0.070	0.075
20–24	2	0.682	0.650	1.332	0.076	0.076	0.143	0.111	0.103	0.107
25–29	3	1.406	1.350	2.756	0.197	0.181	0.378	0.140	0.134	0.137
30–34	4	1.981	1.881	3.862	0.307	0.273	0.580	0.155	0.145	0.150
35–39	5	2.343	2.224	4.567	0.392	0.362	0.754	0.167	0.163	0.165
40–44	6	2.734	2.595	5.329	0.499	0.460	0.959	0.183	0.177	0.180
45–49	7	3.097	2.951	6.048	0.667	0.591	1.258	0.215	0.200	0.208

Author Index

Subject Index